HAUNTED
CHESTER

HAUNTED
CHESTER

DAVID BRANDON

The
History
Press

First published 2008

The History Press Ltd
The Mill, Brimscombe Port
Stroud, Gloucestershire, GL5 2QG
www.thehistorypress.co.uk

Reprinted 2009, 2010, 2011

British Library Cataloguing in Publication Data.
A catalogue record for this book is available from the British Library.

ISBN 978 0 7524 4781 0

Typesetting and origination by The History Press Ltd.
Printed in Great Britain

CONTENTS

INTRODUCTION
GHOSTS AND OTHER
SPOOKY SPECTRES

The ultimate mystery of life is what happens to us when we die. Is the vital spark, the soul that makes each of us distinctive individuals, simply snuffed out only to be followed immediately by the decay of our physical parts? Most of us are uncomfortable with the idea that the world with which we are so familiar continues after we have died and particularly that it can apparently cope perfectly well without us. How much better it is to hope or believe that something awaits us; that there is indeed an afterlife. Such a possibility, however, is viewed by most of us with a mixture of fascination and trepidation.

Many of the world's religions are preoccupied with the issue of the continued existence of our souls after physical death. Indeed, some religions teach that this life is merely a preparation for the next and that we will all be judged by the Almighty when we die. Such religions have created elaborate codes of dos and don'ts which we ignore – literally – at our peril if we want to ensure that we are given a favourable appraisal at the time of our death.

Most religions have created destinations for the souls of the departed. In the case of Christianity these are Heaven, the place for the good where arrivals can expect to enjoy a perpetual idyllic existence, and Hell, a state of continuous unpleasant experiences for those who have given themselves over to a life of sin. Some Christians believe in a kind of half-way house called Purgatory. Here the souls of 'the not completely good but not hopelessly bad' are lodged while they are called to account and atone for their unredeemed misdemeanours. If all goes well, they will in due course graduate to Heaven.

If it is thought that our souls live on in another world, then it is only a small step to visualise the dead returning to the living world on certain occasions and under certain conditions. In many cultures, it has long been believed that the dead yearn to return to the scenes of their earthly lives and that they bitterly resent and envy those who they knew and who are still alive. The soul therefore comes back – often angry and seeking revenge, perhaps on someone who wronged it while it was alive. Maybe it wants to settle the hash of the person who murdered it. At the very least it feels the need to find some way of making its feelings known to the still-living.

On occasions the soul is apparently a trifle confused, but appears to want to sort things out that were left unresolved or somehow unsatisfactory when its owner died, such perhaps as the manner or place of the body's burial. The soul may return if its bodily remains are disturbed or treated with a lack of respect. It may return to provide a warning to the living concerning their behaviour or perhaps an impending disaster. A prime time for a re-appearance is on the anniversary of its death. Sometimes, perhaps, the soul comes back simply out of curiosity. Some seem intent on returning and continuing to perform the habitual actions they undertook when they were still alive. Yet others act as if they want to atone for the sins they committed.

When it returns, the soul is said to be a ghost. These have both fascinated and frightened mankind for thousands of years.

There are many ways in which ghostly phenomena manifest themselves. They may be seen or heard. Often though, people claiming to have had such experiences say that they have 'sensed' their activity or presence rather than having had a more tangible, easily described contact. Perhaps they have smelt the stench of bodily corruption or experienced a sudden and literally chilling fall in the temperature around them. Unexplained footfalls; items rearranged without any apparent agency; disembodied sighs and groans; things that go bump in the night. All these and a host of other unexplained phenomena feature in the continuous flow of reports made by people who claim to have had or think they may have had encounters with ghosts or other supernatural phenomena. Many of these witnesses are not suggestible, are not attention-seekers and in some cases may even be positively stolid and unimaginative. A person talking about the ghostly experiences he or she has had may well incur ridicule. Being the butt of mockery makes most people feel uncomfortable. For this reason it is likely that many unexplained phenomena go unreported and therefore unpublicised.

Some of the stories are what might be called serial hauntings, with the same ghost being seen, heard or sensed in or around the same location by many people over a long period. Chester has a fair number of these. Other ghosts have made single or at best fleeting appearances – perhaps they completed the purpose for which they came back and, having no further business in this world, returned whence they came. No one has ever given a fully satisfactory explanation of why it seems that they appear to some people but not others in the same place at the same time.

The 'ghosts' may not even be the returning souls of humans. Ghostly phenomena associated with cats, dogs and horses, for example, also feature in such reports. This raises the fascinating conundrum of whether animals, like humans, have souls which outlive their physical deaths. Some religions would regard such a claim as quite preposterous. If we accept ghostly animals as well as humans, it is worth noting that they generally seem to be of animals with which humans have much contact and with which they can build close and often fond relationships. Cats, dogs and even ducks are examples. Somebody can put us right, but we've yet to come across a ghost story in this country involving a rat or an adder, for example, these being creatures to which there is a general aversion.

Children's fictional stories may have ghosts covered in white sheets, rattling chains and emitting screeching noises. In adult fiction the ghosts are usually more subtle. In the works of that doyen of ghost-story writers, M.R. James, the ghosts are little more than hints or suggestions. In spite of being so understated, they are capable of being extraordinarily menacing and malevolent. Truly the icy finger tracing down the spine.

Belief in ghosts is almost as old as the human race. Ghostly phenomena continue to exert a perennial interest even in the modern world dominated by the rationalities associated with the knowledge and use of science and technology; with a secular, materialist world deeply imbued with scepticism and cynicism. Even today in the twenty-first century, a house reputed to be haunted may be difficult to sell. Each year priests carry out innumerable exorcisms, in all seriousness intended to bring peace to the living and repose to the spirits of the dead.

Something primeval, some vestigial sixth sense causes the tiny hairs to rise on the back of the neck at certain times and in certain places. Frissons of disquietude verging on fright or sometimes even on terror may cause a rash of goose pimples for reasons we simply cannot explain. We love mysteries and we love to be comfortably scared. All of us are fascinated by photographs or clips of film purporting to show ghostly phenomena. Ghosts are big business. Films and books dealing with fictional ghosts enjoy great popularity, as do books and walks highlighting the paranormal phenomena of many of Britain's towns and cities. Spiritualism and psychical research are going strong and still trying to obtain incontrovertible evidence to sink the sceptics. Ghosts remain as much a part of popular culture as they were in the Middle Ages.

Do ghosts exist? If so, what are they? Do they have any objective existence or are they simply the product of superstitious minds, personal susceptibility or overheated imagination? If we accept the claims of serious people to have had experiences of a supernatural kind, what was it that they actually saw, heard or otherwise sensed? Isn't there a common-sense explanation for most or all of these phenomena? Even if we do not wish to probe too deeply into these questions, most of us can still appreciate a spooky story or movie, can keenly anticipate the thrill of jumping out of our skins at the appropriate moment on a ghost walk or simply take pleasure in finding out about the phantoms and spectres of the place where we live. They are part of the rich and fascinating tapestry of folklore, legend and fact that is local history.

One theory of haunting is that ghostly phenomena are a kind of spiritual film, a force generated in places where deeds of violence or great emotional upheavals have taken place. An energy is released which replicates at least some of the sights and sounds of those powerful events. This energy is then infused into the places concerned and allows the re-enactment of these events to be experienced from time to time by the still-living or at least those people who are receptive to supernatural or psychic phenomena. If there is any substance to this theory, it does account for the disappearance of some habitual and long-established ghosts. The highly charged emotional ether simply dissipates over time.

If you ask people what kinds of places they expect to be haunted, their responses would probably include 'Gothick' semi-derelict mansions worthy of the Addams Family; the crypts of ancient churches; hoary, ivy-clad old ruins; dank and dingy castle dungeons; crossroads where the bodies of highwaymen used to hang in chains suspended from gibbets and also the local 'lover's leap', the scene over the years of tragic suicides provoked by the miseries of unrequited love. To some extent such scenarios are clichés. This spiritual film idea, if it has any plausibility, helps to explain why the locations where ghosts are reported are often essentially everyday and mundane.

The Chester district has more than its fair share of ancient buildings and also of numerous locations boasting consistent reports of spooky happenings. By no means do all of them fit into the mould of the cliché. Some of the places and sites to be reviewed are remarkable only in their ordinariness – even if the happenings associated with them are anything but ordinary. They include pubs, shops, offices and suburban semi-detached houses of the 1930s. The people who have experienced the ghostly phenomena are the people we would never even glance at as we pass them in the street going about their everyday business. Most are too concerned with the issues of getting on with living in the twenty-first century to go around actively looking for paranormal experiences. Across the country as a whole, it is likely that over a third of the population will admit, perhaps a little shamefacedly, to believing in ghosts. As many as 15 per cent of the population claims to have had experiences which they thought had something to do with ghosts.

The lack of scientifically assembled, rigorously documented and unassailable evidence concerning ghosts only acts to titillate our interest and imagination. Were the Loch Ness Monster to be captured and put on permanent show, it is likely that after an initial burst of excited, even fervent attention, there would be a slow ebbing although probably never a total lapse of interest. It would be a bit like the zoo: somewhere to take the children and, much later on in life, the grandchildren, but not a place you visit too often. The same can probably be said for ghosts. One in captivity readily available for all to see would rob ghosts of much of their interest, their mystique, their perennial attraction.

I am a social and cultural historian. This means that I am interested in all manifestations of popular culture and want to record, analyse and attempt to explain their significance. Interest in and alleged experience of ghostly activity is as old as humanity itself and therefore is very much within the purview of social history. It is not necessary as a historian that I should believe or indeed disbelieve in ghosts. I do think that some honestly presented reports of strange phenomena have unknown but entirely mundane explanations. People subjected to experiences evoking extreme emotions such as terror may not be reliable witnesses. Some reports are made by people seeking attention and publicity – a brief few days of celebrity. Others are by deliberate hoaxers or those with an overactive imagination. It is even possible that some reports have been made by those so bored by their employment that they have tried to enliven the workplace by inventing stories of paranormal happenings.

I have no axe to grind. In what follows, I describe and sometimes attempt to comment on or amplify information that has come my way. I acknowledge that in a few cases readers may discern that I think someone is trying to pull a fast one. A historian needs to question, even to be sceptical of the information and evidence that comes his way, and nowhere is this truer than in reports of supernatural activity. In my opinion social history should be informative, stimulating and fun. Historians need to have a sense of humour. I admit to having fun getting this material together and I hope it shows.

For those who make a serious study of psychic phenomena, I am aware that in this book I make technically imprecise use of words like 'ghost', 'haunting', 'phantom', 'spectre', 'poltergeist' and so on. I can only apologise to the experts for this while believing that the terminology used here is adequate for the general reader.

The names of pubs and shops can change overnight. As far as I know, the names of such businesses given here are correct as of the time of writing.

The ghostly and other associated phenomena described in this book come from a variety of sources including many local people who have been kind enough to contact the author about their experiences. To all of them, I offer sincere thanks. I would also like to thank the staff of the Chester City Library, the Tourist Information Centre and the Chester Heritage Centre for their enthusiastic and generous help. My son, Ed Brandon, has taken the photographs and provided valuable advice. My thanks go to him.

CHESTER
A BRIEF HISTORICAL
SURVEY

Chester is without doubt a very special place. Located on a sandstone spur overlooking the River Dee before it broadens out into its wide estuary, it teems with ancient buildings and historical associations. Chester owes its ancient importance to its geographical location with what used to be the lowest safe crossing point on the River Dee and as a major port for North-West England and the North Midlands. Also defining the city was its strategic placement athwart the main access routes to and from much of North Wales. The fertile Cheshire Plain is nearby.

Its strategic position has invested the city's history with centuries of bloody strife and turbulence. Chester has witnessed sieges, battles, riots and other civil disturbances and these have all contributed to making it a place with the antiquities, associations and atmosphere to attract huge numbers of visitors and tourists. Not that Chester is simply a museum storing up reminders of the past. It has done well in that difficult task, always replete with pitfalls, which tries to bring together in some semblance of harmony a celebration of the best of the past with the requirements of the modern world. Chester manages to be a lively, prosperous place that is a pleasure for people to live and work in and which is also an attraction for the many folk from elsewhere who visit for a wide variety of purposes. These could include so-called 'retail therapy', leisure and recreation, culture and entertainment and fascination with the city's history and heritage.

It is likely that the Romans established a small base at Chester initially in the late AD 50s. This was followed by a large, permanent fort about AD 79. The Romans gave the place the name Deva or Castra Devana meaning something like 'The Divine' and referring to the River Dee which both they and their native predecessors would have held as sacred. The Romans gave Chester a street pattern which, so far as the city centre is concerned, remains remarkably intact to this day. The defensive ramparts were roughly rectangular in shape and running through the military settlement on an east to west orientation was the Via Principalis, marked today by Eastgate and Watergate Streets. The military headquarters were located on the Via Principalis at the point where it was joined by the Via Decumana which was the road in from the north which is now called Northgate Street. They met at the spot now known as The Cross. A lesser street went south from the intersection, forming what has evolved into Bridge Street and Lower Bridge Street. It was the Roman's Via Praetoria.

Masonry walls were built to strengthen the fortifications around AD 200. Deva developed into a sizeable and sophisticated Roman garrison, host over the years to several crack legions. Their main function was to guard the lush and fertile agricultural lands of Cheshire from marauding Welsh raiding parties as well as to make forays into Wales attempting to keep the Welsh in their place. Chester became the base for perhaps as many as 6,000 soldiers who were supported with all the amenities and leisure facilities needed to make a tour of duty at this far-flung part of the empire more tolerable for men who were likely to have been brought up in far balmier and more congenial climes, many hundreds of miles away. These facilities included baths, temples, theatres, taverns – and, of course, brothels – all of which would have provided that little something that helped to make the off-duty hours more bearable in what the soldiers must have thought was a pretty barbaric part of the world. The presence of this garrison and the business opportunities that it offered, both open and often illicit, attracted camp-followers from among the indigenous population, many of whom lived in a suburb developed just to the east, outside the gates.

The complex processes that constitute historical development demonstrate that nothing is permanent in this world. Although the Romans had engaged in a process of constantly improving the settlement of Deva and its defences, the empire of which they were a part increasingly experienced both internal decay and sustained external attack. These became so serious that in the late fourth century, the legion on duty at the time was urgently recalled for what proved an ultimately futile attempt to defend those parts of the Roman Empire its ruling elements regarded as considerably more crucial than the borders of Wales. '*Sic transit gloria mundi*'. Deva, along with many other Roman settlements that we marvel at today for the highly civilized living standards and conditions they must have given their favoured occupants, fell into rack and ruin. Those who occupied the area after the Romans left had a different culture which had little use for towns, but Chester's strategic position ensured that events did not pass it by and the Britons and Saxons fought each other in the vicinity. The Celts called it Caerleon while the Saxons preferred Lagaceaster, both names meaning something like 'city of the legions'.

Around 616 King Aethelfrith of Northumbria gained a great victory over the Britons close by. It is said that a sequel to this was the massacre of about 2,000 monks. The Chester area was occupied by the Saxons at least from the middle of the seventh century but was apparently deserted in 893 when a Danish army camped within the walls and used the site as a base for attacks on Mercia. Extensive repairs and improvements were made to the defensive works in about 907 whereupon Chester seems to have settled into two roles which it still enjoys, those of regional centre and county town of the area which became known as Cheshire.

In 973 Edgar, who had been crowned 'King of All England', is supposed to have sailed round the Welsh coast and up the River Dee as far as Chester to his palace on the south bank of the river. Legend says that he then had eight vassal kings row him across the Dee and back in a public display of submission. He is supposed to have steered the boat himself, symbolically showing that he guided the destinies of all these subject kings and their realms. There is, or was, a rather nice tiled mural depicting this event in the Bull & Stirrup pub in Northgate.

Even before the Normans arrived, Chester – or Cestre, as it had become – was a thriving port, the defensive capability of its walls fully restored and the first bridge had been built. With a population probably of about 3,000, it was one of the largest towns of Saxon England.

The Normans found the natives of North-West England a truculent lot and the latter were only put in their place after William brutally crushed an attempted uprising in 1069. Chester was taken by the Normans in 1070 and William then placed it in the hands of one of the few men he seems to have totally trusted. This was Hugh Lupus, who became Earl of Chester. He was William's nephew and a man of the same ruthlessly efficient sort as the Conqueror himself. The task he faced was no easy one. William had given him virtual autonomy over a region stretching from the River Clwyd as far north as the estuary of the Ribble in what is now Lancashire. The Welsh refused to roll over and submit gracefully, causing him and his successors enormous problems over the years. Chester's importance was growing rapidly. Hugh Lupus built the castle as his main military and administrative base and he also founded a Benedictine monastery then dedicated to St Werburgh which provides the nucleus of the present cathedral. The Blackfriars (Dominicans), Whitefriars (Carmelites) and Greyfriars (Franciscans) all established bases in the thirteenth century in what was clearly a very prosperous city at the time. Lesser-known (and short-lived) were the Friars of the Sack.

Chester's strategic position was exploited to the full during Edward I's campaigns against the Welsh at the end of the thirteenth century. It was his chief operational base and became prosperous because of the constant presence of large numbers of soldiers and the supplies and munitions associated with war, many of which came through the port, located close to where the Roodee now is. Military issues apart, Chester was the main port for Ireland and was also engaged in seagoing trade with various provinces in France and Spain.

All this hustle and bustle and the wealth associated with it had to be enjoyed while it lasted. In the fourteenth century the city's prosperity began to wane because the campaigns against the Welsh were run down but most of all because little could be done to prevent the Dee from silting up. Along with the rest of England, Chester's hinterland was badly affected by the fall-out from the Black Death. Things worsened in the fifteenth century during which time the decline of trade and a number of fires meant that the city became full of derelict buildings. In the early sixteenth century, grass was growing in the streets. Three friaries and the nunnery were closed in 1536 during the Dissolution of the Monasteries but at least the great Abbey of St Werburgh's was spared and became a cathedral and the centre of an enormous new diocese then stretching as far as Cumberland and North Yorkshire.

A gradual recovery in Chester's fortunes began in the sixteenth century but in keeping with a local tradition for making such tactical errors, the city backed the wrong side in the English Civil War. Initially, the influential local landowner Sir William Brereton announced the city's support for the Parliamentary cause but this was bitterly opposed by the local people who were devoted to King Charles I and had to be restrained from lynching Brereton. The outcome was that Chester became an important centre of the Royalist cause and its strategic situation meant that Chester played a very significant part in the war. It underwent a lengthy siege in late 1644 and through to early 1646. The valour of the soldiers and citizenry was recognized when Chester was allowed by the besieging Parliamentary forces to surrender with honour, which it did on 3 February 1646. The price to pay was a city which had been physically and mentally battered. It is said that the townsfolk had been forced to eat dogs, cats and rats in the latter days of the siege. No sooner had a start been made on returning to normality than there was an outbreak of bubonic plague which killed roughly a quarter of the population. Once more the locals, who must have been wondering what else Fate could throw at them, buckled down to yet another attempt to revive and develop the local economy.

Engineering work in the mid-eighteenth century produced a new channel or canal joining Chester to the Dee estuary at Connagh's Quay and this did something to restore the city's fortunes, at least for a while. Exports included coal, lead and salt and the renowned Cheshire cheese. An uphill and losing battle was fought against the shifting silt of the Dee and for a time Chester developed and controlled what in effect were outports in the Wirral such as Parkgate, Neston and Heswall. The transhipment of goods and their transport overland was, however, costly. In the nineteenth century, ships became larger and larger and Liverpool with its deeper water facilities gained an unassailable advantage over Chester. Although some smaller ocean-going vessels were still being manoeuvred by tugs from Saltney to the Crane Wharf as late as the 1880s, the city had no option but to abandon its pretensions to being a port. All was not lost, however. Chester started to become a fashionable place to live with elegant brick-built houses for the well-heeled and the kind of social facilities (such as assembly rooms) required by its better-off citizens and the Cheshire county set which made the city a centre of their activities. Over the decades it carved out a role for itself as a social and ecclesiastical centre, county and assizes town, venue for horse-racing, market for its rural hinterland and, in the nineteenth and twentieth centuries, as a place noted for high-class shopping and an attraction for tourists.

In many respects Chester was like Bath or York. It was an early example of a town largely given over to what is now called the service industry. Like Bath, large-scale industrial development in the late eighteenth and the nineteenth centuries mostly passed it by. Chester ceased to be a port of any significance, but became first a significant coaching town, a canal port and then an important railway centre. What industries Chester did develop tended to be related to the agricultural nature of the surrounding area. It grew much less rapidly than many manufacturing towns in south-east Lancashire and the West Midlands, for example, but it developed in prosperity and importance in the role it was carving out for itself.

The fortifications built by the Romans are about two miles in length and although altered and reconstructed many times over the centuries, they are one of the glories of Chester and provide a marvellous promenade from which to view many of the city's attractions. Among Chester's glories are its abundant Roman remains and new antiquities of that age frequently come to light, particularly during construction works. The world-famous Rows, formerly more extensive, are unique and charming two-tiered shopping arcades of medieval origin. They draw visitors in huge numbers, many of whom also gaze in awe at the apparently ancient half-timbered 'magpie' buildings in the centre without realizing that they mostly date from the Victorian period. Over 90 per cent of the apparently half-timbered black and white buildings are in fact products of the nineteenth century or early twentieth century and the buildings are mainly not half-timbered at all. The wooden beams and other features are frequently nailed on (although not obviously so), and it would be curmudgeonly to deny that the magpie buildings impart an attractive character to Chester. These black and white buildings form a delightful contrast with the warm red sandstone of the city walls and many of Chester's other older main buildings. Under several of the ancient buildings in the centre are fine medieval crypts, many of which house shops or eating places and can therefore easily be viewed by the public.

Chester is a fascinating hotchpotch of architectural styles. It is not surprising that a city with such a diverse, colourful, turbulent and sometimes bloody history and heritage lays claim to being one of Britain's most haunted locations. There are even claims that it is the most haunted place outside London – though it is difficult to know just how 'hauntedness' can be measured or quantified.

What follows is a description of many of Chester's reported supernatural phenomena and of the location from which those reports have come. The inclusion of all, or any, of them must not be taken as evidence of an evaluation or judgement about their authenticity on the part of the author. He is an historian. The task of an historian is 'not to weep, not to laugh but to understand'. The author is very aware of the widespread and persistent interest throughout history in the strange and often inexplicable experiences brought together in the category of the 'supernatural'. These experiences have happened so often and taken so many forms that it would be unprofessional not to take them seriously. This book is intended to be informative and, hopefully, entertaining. It is hoped that it may encourage readers to further study of local history, topography, folklore and the paranormal.

It is always difficult to decide on the best way of organizing and presenting a book which brings together stories of ghosts and spooks with the topography and history of a particular town, city or district. In this book, the places in central Chester having supernatural associations are numbered in the text.

The central area of the city is divided into three parts, starting with that in the north-west. That is the area demarcated by the west side of Northgate Street from The Cross, Northgate to the line of the city walls to the Watergate and the north side of Watergate Street and back to The Cross. The second is embraced by The Cross, the south side of Watergate Street to the Watergate, the city walls round to the Old Dee Bridge, up the west side of Lower Bridge Street and Bridge Street to The Cross. The third section consists of that part of Chester within the walls to the east of Northgate, Bridge Street and Lower Bridge Street plus a little extramural Chester in the area of The Groves and St John's church. A fourth section deals with an assortment of ghosts and associated phenomena in outer Chester, and finally there is a brief examination of some similar reports from the region surrounding Chester.

An itinerary taking in some of the more interesting sites (and other sights) is offered at the end of the book as is a bibliography of sources and suggested further reading.

GHOSTS GALORE

The George and Dragon

There is of course a natural affinity between ghosts and spirits, so where better to start than with a pub? In this case the pub is the George and Dragon, which stands in Upper Northgate Street at the intersection of Parkgate Road and Liverpool Road outside and just to the north of the city walls. It is a listed and impressive building with a half-timbered black and white frontage of typical Chester style. It loosely copies the late medieval or Tudor style because, like so many others in Chester, the building is actually Victorian. One slightly mocking name sometimes given to such buildings is 'Brewer's Tudor'.

The George and Dragon.

The pub stands on the site of an old Roman cemetery which was located by the main road leaving Chester for the north. The ghostly manifestation takes the form of the sound of regular massed footsteps making exactly the kind of noise one would expect of Roman soldiers on the march. Nothing is ever seen, but witnesses have described how they have heard the footsteps approaching, going past and then fading away into the distance, apparently oblivious of any physical barriers (such as walls) that they might encounter on the way. This raises the question as to whether we are talking about one ghost or many. Is it the sound of one or more of the inhabitants of the burial ground who refuse to lie down?

Reports of this phenomenon have been made for many years, and it, or they – whatever is producing this rather uncanny noise – is no respecter of such niceties as modern licensing hours and manifests itself as and when the whim takes it. The footsteps have been heard pacing across the upper floor of the pub, from one end to the other, in the witching hours of the night. Having marched in one direction, they tramp back in the opposite direction about twenty minutes later. The George and Dragon offers bed and breakfast, so anyone who wants to take the chance of being kept awake by the incorporeal tread of marching Roman troops only need to book in for an overnight stay.

Bridge of Sighs

This curious structure spans the deep cutting built in the 1770s containing the Shropshire Union Canal close to the Northgate and its name, somewhat ironically, makes a reference to the bridge in Venice connecting the Doge's Palace with the nearby prison. Over this bridge passed prisoners who had been

The Bridge of Sighs.

The Northgate.

condemned to death in the Doge's court and who were making their solemn and forlorn way to the place of execution. Architecturally, the two bridges are not in the same league. The Chester Bridge of Sighs originally had railings: this is just as well, because otherwise the prisoners would have added dizziness and danger to their other woes.

Across Chester's own 'Bridge of Sighs' similar gloomy little processions once made their way from the gaol in Northgate to the Chapel of St John in the Bluecoat School where the prisoners uttered their orisons and tried to make their peace with the Almighty. Apparently these processions are sometimes re-enacted in spectral form. Over the years people claim to have heard noises in this vicinity. They have ascribed these sounds to having been present when one of these re-enactments is taking place. Nothing is ever seen, which is just as well because the ghosts concerned would need a good head for heights if they were to avoid plummeting into the canal. It has to be said that these witnesses have done little for their credibility in that when asked about the sounds they have heard in the vicinity of the bridge they have described them as being 'like sighs'.

Close by the Bridge of Sighs, in the vicinity of the Northgate and also associated with the former gaol, muffled thumps have been heard on windy nights. These noises are said to be the result of the corpses of executed felons who were hanged in chains and then suspended from gibbets which then banged against nearby walls.

Above and left: The Goblin Tower.

The gaol itself was originally housed in the large medieval Northgate which remained in place until its demolition in 1808. By the time of its closure the Northgate was widely regarded as being an especially bad example of a working prison. The well-respected penal reformer John Howard, visiting in 1787, described it as a 'disgrace to such an opulent city'. In 1807 it was replaced by a new prison not far away on the site of what was later the Queen's School.

With all the human misery that the Northgate Gaol must have seen, it is hardly to be wondered at that supernatural phenomena have apparently made their presence felt nearby even after it was pulled down. The gaol contained a minute, windowless cell so small that even an average-sized occupant would be doubled-up in a foetal position enduring unspeakable agony if condemned to remain there for more than a few minutes. It is said that at very quiet times, which in this bustling part of the city means the early hours of the morning, moans and cries of despair can be heard supposedly coming from this cell (which was filled up with rubble when the gaol was pulled down).

Morgan's Mount

On the ancient city walls in the north of the city close, just east of where they cross St Martins Way, stands Morgan's Mount. This part of the city's defences saw considerable action during the prolonged siege of Chester by Parliamentary forces in 1645 to 1646. The eponymous Morgan is supposed to have been a junior Royalist officer who commanded a battery at this point. From time to time spectral Royalist soldiers have been seen. Presumably they have the flowing hair, frills and furbelows and the generally foppish appearance popularly associated with the fighting men who supported Charles I. These contrast sharply with the severe, even austere clothes of their Parliamentary opponents. Both characterizations are in fact caricatures.

Goblin Tower or Pemberton's Parlour

Close by Morgan's Mount is another tower on the walls known as Pemberton's Parlour – or curiously, as the Goblin Tower or Mount. This was originally a circular tower straddling the walls, remodelled as a semi-circular tower around 1700 and undergoing a further reconstruction in 1894. Apparently Pemberton was a rope-maker who used to ascend to the tower and watch his men working – or perhaps not working – in the yard below.

On occasions ghostly but flamboyantly dressed cavalier gentlemen and their equally showy ladies are seen walking the city walls hereabouts.

The Water Tower

The history of the River Dee could be said to be a tale of silt and sand. At one time the river lapped the walls the Romans erected at the north-western extremity of their garrison town. Over the centuries, however, silt built up under the walls at this point which left the oddly-named Bonewaldestnorne's Tower some small distance from the tidal basin in which Chester's considerable seaborne commercial traffic loaded and unloaded. Chester's prosperity may have owed much to its maritime connections but these also made the city vulnerable to attack by pirates and other raiders coming up the Dee.

Bonewaldestnorne's Tower.

It was decided that a new tower commanding a more effective view over the port area and the river approaches was needed, and in 1322 the New, or Water, Tower was erected for this purpose. This was built at the end of a linking wall from Bonewaldestnorne's Tower and was well-designed for its purpose.

Obviously it was necessary for a sharp lookout to be kept at all times. A ghostly figure has been seen on many occasions around this tower and some say that it belongs to a rather wayward sentinel who, bored with his duties as nothing ever seemed to happen, decided to take unofficial leave of absence and went off for a tumble in the arms of his beloved. Now whether he was executed for this dereliction of duty we shall never know, but the belief in certain circles is that the ghost is the negligent watchman who is being made to pay for putting the pleasures of the flesh above his duty.

Close by in the Water Tower Gardens, buried under the sward, is a plague pit. Chester experienced several appalling visitations of the bubonic plague. This pit is said to contain the remains of about 2,000 victims of one of these epidemics and it is hardly surprising that loud wails of dismay are said to have been heard in the vicinity.

Water Tower from the city walls.

Water Tower.

Steps to the plague pit.

Old Chester Royal Infirmary

Close to and inside the north-west corner of the city walls is the Old Chester Royal Infirmary, founded in 1755. A most unusual ghost frequently witnessed in this somewhat forbidding edifice is that of 'Soldier McKenzie'. He was a member of a Scottish regiment who was seriously wounded in action in the First World War and was brought to this hospital for treatment. Unfortunately he died of his injuries and was buried in the standard hospital shroud rather than in his distinctive regimental uniform (complete with the kilt) of which he and his comrades were so proud. His spirit has clearly been unable to take such an insult lying down and so he roams the building engaged in a futile search for his full regimentals. Those who have seen him say that he is apparently totally preoccupied with this task and that he evinces no interest whatever in the living denizens of the building.

The site of the Royal Infirmary is now desirable inner-city apartments. In view of the change of use for his surroundings, has 'Soldier McKenzie' given up the ghost?

Queen's School

On City Walls Road stands the Queen's School, founded in 1878. Externally, this building looks tailor-made for the housing of supernatural happenings. Internally, it has exactly the right creaking floors, rickety staircases and small, secretive and sinister-looking attic rooms. Over the years there have been reports of the door to the music room opening and closing without any apparent human agency. Many pupils have witnessed this phenomenon and it was so regular and they became so nonchalant about it that, in defiance of their teachers, they would pipe up and say 'hello' to the invisible being when it opened the door and came into the room. The door would always close after exactly the right brief interval that would have allowed a person to enter the room and close the door behind it. Is this a ghost or could it be a poltergeist?

No. 102 Watergate Street

No. 102 Watergate Street is the scenario for disconcerting and inexplicable noises and chilling blasts of cold air which mean that no one wants to live there. It provides office accommodation.

Near The Cross in The Rows stands the Victoria pub. An ancient building, it has traded as licensed premises for several centuries, but only recently have paranormal phenomena been reported. Admittedly, they are pretty low key: members of staff have reported touches by unseen hands, odd hissings and whisperings and items moved around for no good purpose and apparently without human agency. As will be seen, this kind of thing is very much the norm for the pubs in Chester city centre.

Town Hall

The city fathers of Chester were all of a dither in 1862 when the Exchange burnt down. This building, dating back to 1698, had acted as a Town Hall. Should it be rebuilt, or could the fire provide the opportunity to erect a brand new Town Hall, consonant with what they considered to be the dignity and importance of the city? The decision was taken to go for a new building. The usual procedure in those

Burial ground over the plague pit.

Royal Infirmary.

The Queen's School.

Front door of No. 102 Watergate Street.

days was to make a public announcement in the national newspapers stating what was being proposed and inviting architects to submit designs. This was in effect a competition, and the successful architect was the little-known William Henry Lynn of Belfast.

The foundation stone was laid with due ceremony in 1865 and the building officially declared open with even more ceremony by the Prince of Wales, one of whose other titles was, appropriately, 'Earl of Chester'. He, of course, was the future Edward VII. The date was 14 October 1869.

The building is an impressive one, visible over much of the city because of its tower, which is 160ft high. The Town Hall can be loosely described as Neo-Gothic, perhaps with a dash of Venetian, and is of grey ashlared sandstone. It stands where the Romans had the hospital or valetudinarium for their garrison. How many legionnaires died there of disease or injuries sustained in battle? Part of the Town Hall became a police station, and so a later macabre association goes back only as far as 1966 when the infamous 'Moors Murderers', Ian Brady and Myra Hindley, were held there in underground cells while they stood trial at Chester Assizes.

Chester Town Hall.

With the site being such an ancient one is it is hardly surprising that it qualifies for inclusion in a work on Chester's ghosts. The Town Hall currently houses the Tourist Information Centre and in recent years several of the staff have sensed an invisible but menacing presence while they have been at work. There has been nothing really tangible, but they have traced the source of whatever it is to a storeroom under the grand external staircase on the front of the building where it looks over Town Hall Square. At least one member of staff claimed to have encountered something lurking in this storeroom, but unfortunately chose never to elaborate on what it was.

Cleaning staff working in the lobby of the Town Hall at the top of this staircase have reported feeling very uncomfortable, feeling a presence and thinking, but never being sure, that they had seen something out of their corner of their eyes. This happened at times when the public are not admitted to the building.

Town Hall steps.

The Coach House

Some stories with supernatural associations are very difficult to define or make any sense of. On the same side of Northgate Street, close to the Town Hall, stands the Coach House pub, long known as the Coach and Horses. It is a reconstruction of an old building dating back to the seventeenth century – and it is the scene of a slightly unnerving story of the paranormal kind.

It was the evening of a summer's day in 1988. An elderly man walked in, looking as if he had the weight of the world on his shoulders. He bought a drink, retired to a seat by himself and sat staring gloomily into space. He looked so woebegone that the kind-hearted barmaid asked him if anything was wrong. Although he was not looking for pity, he admitted that his wife had died recently after a long and happy marriage. The conversation fizzled out, but the man booked a room for bed and breakfast, completing the register in the normal way. He then told her he was going out for a walk round the streets before it was time to turn in for a good night's sleep. Closing time came and went and when the man did not return, the puzzled and concerned landlord informed the police. They checked with the police in Birkenhead (which was the man's home town). The police went to the address the man had given. Another family was now in residence: they said that they had lived there

The Coach House.

for a few years and knew nothing about the man. It was a different matter when they talked to the neighbours: some of them remembered him clearly. His wife had indeed died – but it was eight years ago! The man was so devastated by her death that he went into a sudden decline and died just one week after!

So who was the man in the bar of the Coach and Horses that warm summer's night in 1988?

King's Buildings

King Street is off the west side of Northgate and at one time was known as Barn Lane because it led to a tithe barn associated with St Werburgh's Abbey. King's Buildings consist of a terrace of heavily restored Georgian houses originally built in 1776. A woman lay in bed feeling very poorly and seemingly unable to make any improvement. One day she was visited by what she said was a ghostly doctor in the costume of the seventeenth century. Such an experience might have finished some people off, but not this woman. The spectral figure had touched her on the forehead and she went on to make a quick recovery from her indisposition.

King's Buildings.

The Pied Bull

Northgate Street attracts those who like a pint or two because, although some former hostelries are now used for other purposes, there are still several licensed premises and one or two of them are of considerable historic character. A cattle market was formerly in this area and its presence was reflected in the names of a number of hostelries hereabouts, including the Pied Bull and the Bull and Stirrup (which stands just outside the North Gate).

The Pied Bull exudes historical atmosphere. It has an eighteenth-century frontage built over the pavement. This frontage disguises an older building, behind which was once a town residence known as the 'Bull Mansion'. It is claimed to be the oldest continuously serving pub in Chester. Part of the interior fabric dates to the sixteenth and seventeenth centuries and there is a splendid, marvellously gnarled and well-used wooden staircase of the seventeenth century. Under this staircase is a door leading down to the cellar. Many of the pub's landlords over the years have experienced a sudden and strong blast of chilly air – chillier than the mere coolness expected of a pub cellar.

Only in recent years has a possible explanation for this rather unnerving phenomenon emerged. A local historian undertaking research in the archives of the Chester Coroners unearthed a report from 1690 describing the fate of one John Davies. On the 27 September of that year he apparently fell down the stairs leading to the cellar. It is unclear what actually happened, although it is stated

The Pied Bull.

that he was carrying a knife. He expired at about two o'clock in the morning. Is this sudden and short-lived gust of cold air anything to do with this unfortunate event or is there some perfectly sensible everyday explanation?

In 2005 a couple stayed in room nine and the man took a photograph of his female companion – or at least, so he thought. When the film was developed, an indistinct something or somebody was shown standing close to her. The couple had been alone in the room when the photograph was taken – or at least, so they thought!

Another manifestation at the Pied Bull is said to be that of a former ostler who went out late one night to check that everything was right with the horses. No one knows how, but he dropped the lantern he was carrying and it broke and ignited the straw. The flames spread so quickly that he could not escape, and he burned to death.

The Red Lion

It seems to be almost *de rigueur* for the pubs on the west side of Northgate Street to be haunted. More than one licensee of the Red Lion has claimed that the cellars of the pub have an unnervingly haunted feel.

The Red Lion.

The Blue Bell Inn

Almost adjacent to the Pied Bull is another, even more ancient building which served as a pub until 1930. It has seen many subsequent uses including (very suitably) an antique shop, and less appropriately a children's boutique by the name of Snow White's. For many years it was the Blue Bell Restaurant, although it has not been a pub for several decades, and its latest incarnation is as East Glory, a restaurant with eastern cuisine. It was first recorded as licensed premises as early as 1494, when it seems to have been called the Bell, but the origins of the building almost certainly predate that time. An odd feature is the way that the pavement of Northgate Street at this point in effect runs through the middle of the building.

On 24 September 1645 a strong Parliamentary force was marching on the city from the south under the leadership of the redoubtable Major-General Sydenham Poyntz. He had reason to believe that the King was in Chester and he knew that if he could strike a quick and successful blow against his forces, enter the city and seize him, the bloody war would be as good as over. Royalist soldiers were quartered in the city in large numbers and they were alerted about the approach of the enemy force. Attack being the best form of defence, it made sense to keep the enemy at bay by riding out to meet them before they got too close to the walls of the city.

Among these soldiers was one young man who for several nights had been enjoying the pleasures of some robust rumpy-pumpy with his young lady friend in one of the bedrooms of the Blue Bell. When word came that a hostile Parliamentary force was approaching the city, he reluctantly tore himself from the warm embraces of his beloved, dressed, drew on his riding boots, clipped on his spurs and rode off, assuring her that he and his comrades-in-arms would give the Roundheads a damned good hiding and that he wouldn't be long returning to take up again where he had been reluctantly forced to leave off.

Windows at the front of the former Blue Bell Inn.

The former Blue Bell Inn.

Battle was joined at Rowton Heath, about three to four miles south-east of Chester. This was where things started to go wrong – it was the Royalists who were on the receiving end of the hiding. More than that – they were given a thorough drubbing, and it was not long before frightened, confused, tired and wounded men began to stream back hoping to find a safe haven behind the city's walls and gates. The young lady looked out for her hero – at first with eager anticipation and then, as time passed, with a growing sense of apprehension.

She has displayed monumental patience: the young man lay dead on the field of battle in 1645, but she is waiting still. One version of the story is that when she realised he was not going to come back, she went down to the cellar and hanged herself. The other account is that she died of a broken heart. It was some years before the haunting started. People working on the premises have seen the apparition of a beautiful young lady dressed in fine clothes of the mid-seventeenth century with a crowning glory consisting of a head of gorgeous blond hair. Her actions seem to consist mainly of approaching and looking out of the left front window on the first floor of the building as if trying to catch a glimpse of her by now seriously belated lover. Members of staff needing to visit the cellar have heard someone softly whispering their name despite the fact that there is no one there to do the whispering. She seems harmless and non-threatening and they accept her presence, which usually makes itself known when dusk is drawing on, with some equanimity. Less happy perhaps are those customers who claim to have seen her while enjoying liquid or more substantial refreshment in the restaurant.

The old fire station.

Old Fire Station, aka 'Chez Jules'

It is somehow typical of Chester that even its fire station in Northgate Street, built and opened in 1911, displays what appears to be fifteenth or sixteenth-century black and white half-timbering with three barge-boarded gables and three rather playful oriel windows of wooden construction.

It closed in 1970 when a new fire station was opened; since then it has been used as a restaurant. This is said to be haunted by the rather fine bearded and moustachioed figure of a fireman in the uniform of several decades ago complete with his brass helmet. Alternatively, he is described as 'unshaven'. When waiting for a call-out, the old hands would regale the rookie fire-fighters with stories about 'Old Jack'. His main activity seems to have been allowing himself to be seen sitting on one of the fire engines and smiling at the observer knowingly and in a rather disconcerting way. 'Old George' was seen doing precisely this by a new fire-fighter who didn't know the ropes at this particular fire station. He was so alarmed at seeing the smiling but rather mirthless apparition that he sounded the alarm – following which, of course, the rest of the watch sprang into action, eager to find out what and where the incident was.

The Ghosts That Never Were

The connection between places that have witnessed events of enormous passion, emotion or tragedy and hauntings has already been commented on. We almost expect such places to provide us with reports about paranormal activity. Some time between AD 607 and 616 a great battle was fought at Chester between the army of King Aethelfrith of Northumbria and a large Welsh force. The Welsh were Christians and they brought with them several hundred monks who they hoped would provide spiritual succour and moral support. Apparently these monks prayed for them as hard as is humanly possible, but did so in vain because the Welsh were utterly defeated.

Needless to say, Aethelfrith was jubilant. An amoral and ruthless man, he loathed and despised Christians. So instead of showing some magnanimity towards his defeated and deflated opponents, he rounded on the monks – who, of course, had not actually done any fighting and had withdrawn some distance from the battle. The problem was that they had been seen praying for all they were worth and Aethelfrith reckoned that was just as bad as actually fighting against him. He had every single one of them slaughtered.

The rage, the fear, the awful pain and the absolute terror unleashed that day so long ago could have been expected to release psychic phenomena, but nothing has ever been reported. Of course it does not help that the exact site of the battle is not known.

UNCANNY
HAPPENINGS OVER IN
THE WEST

The south-west sector of the city within the walls contains another crop of sites with supernatural associations. This is the area demarcated by Watergate Street, Nuns Road, Castle Drive, Lower Bridge Street and Bridge Street.

Watergates Wine Bar

Chester offers a great variety of places for eating and drinking. Many are in ancient buildings or in historic surroundings. This wine bar at Nos 11-15 Watergate Street is in a crypt graced by a fine stone vaulted ceiling.

On occasions a man described as a 'sailor' is sighted rolling though the premises displaying a typically nautical gait, perhaps on his way to or from the former port area of Chester. The descriptions provided by witnesses are rather unhelpful because they omit any useful description of the garb he is wearing. For this reason it is impossible to place this apparition in its time context.

A 'now you see me, now you don't' spectre lurks in Watergate Street itself. Those who claim to have seen it say that it is male and that it appears to be intently looking for somebody or something. If a Good Samaritan tries to approach him to offer help, rather ungratefully the spectre suddenly vanishes. Some have said that that before he disappeared in such a dramatic fashion, the cut of his jib suggested that he was also a sailor. Next time you see a slightly confused, possibly nautical figure in Watergate Street, you might understandably be reluctant to hurry to assist. You could always call out 'Hello, sailor,' but this might be misconstrued by some passers-by.

No. 13 Watergate Street

These premises, currently part of the wine bar, are affected by poltergeist activity. Days or weeks will go by without anything untoward happening and then items for sale will inexplicably be moved around

Watergates Wine Bar.

Watergate Street looking westwards.

No. 13 Watergate Street.

without any visible agency. This is irritating for the staff and more than a trifle disconcerting for those customers who have been present to witness the phenomenon.

Watergate Street is something of a centre of psychic activity. Leche House has a complicated building history with work of all centuries from the fourteenth to the seventeenth. This is supposedly haunted by yet another sailor. Described as 'old-fashioned', this spectre sometimes appears at a first-floor window from which it gazes morosely down on the street below. Leche House contains a priest hole which would have housed fugitive Roman Catholic clerics during the religious troubles of the seventeenth century. A piece of old glass displays evidence of seventeenth-century vandalism. Scratched on it is a graffito with the words 'Charming Miss Oldfield'. How much more seemly a declaration of admiration this is than the kind of thing found daubed on walls these days! The presence of ghostly mariners in Watergate Street could of course be explained by the fact that the street led to the Watergate and the quays, which would have been busy with commerce until the Dee silted up so badly that Chester's days as a port were over.

Other phantoms that sometimes put in an appearance include a young girl wearing clothes of the seventeenth century, a figure believed to be a monk and, more sinister, another monk wearing a cowl which helps to obscure the fact that he has no face.

Stanley Palace.

Stanley Palace

Watergate Street is the least commercialized of the four main streets of Chester that meet at The Cross. As its name suggests, it provided access to the quayside of the thriving medieval port of Chester, the Dee once running much closer to the city walls at this point than it does now.

Close to the junction of Watergate Street and Nicholas Street stands Stanley Palace. This building dates from 1591 and, as its name suggests, it was the town house of the wealthy and powerful Stanley family. It underwent various roles over the years but by the middle of the nineteenth century it was divided into tenements and was badly run down, being in the middle of what had become something of a slum quarter. In 1866 it was bought by the Chester Archaeological Society and then sold to the Earl of Derby in 1889, a condition being that it could not be demolished. In 1928 or 1931, depending on the account, it was presented to the city after having been threatened with demolition – did they really want it? – and in 1935 it was so thoroughly restored that it is hard to tell which bits are original and which date from that time.

Stanley Palace may now look almost too neat and tidy but it fits well into the image the world has of Chester and its black and white buildings. It houses two ghosts. One is a grey lady dressed in the style of the seventeenth century who has been glimpsed wandering rather aimlessly around the Gallery and the Queen Anne Room. She does not seem to exude any particular sense of menace.

The other ghost is believed to be that of James Stanley, 7th Earl of Derby. He was an almost fanatical supporter of the Royalist cause in the English Civil War and in 1651 he paid for his beliefs and actions when he was arrested, tried and found guilty on a charge of treason. He was held in secure confinement in

Stanley Palace before being taken away to be beheaded at Bolton. His ghost is something of an eccentric. It has been seen on many occasions in the rooms on the ground floor and when he decides to manifest himself, which it does on an irregular basis, he chooses to do so apparently wearing a white jacket, black shirt and a darkened face. This has caused him to be described as a very negative ghost.

Stanley Palace has been used as offices for several years by the English Speaking Union.

The Roodee

The River Dee in Roman and medieval times flowed immediately west of the city walls. The river dumped increasing amounts of silt as its profile levelled out and its flow slowed where it approached the estuary. It is probable that long ago the Dee divided at this point and a low island developed between the two arms of the river, that to the east providing access to Chester's port facilities. This low, flat area is of course known as the Roodee, once 'Roodeye'. This means something like 'island of the Rood or Cross'. The legend tells that once a rood stood on the island. It dated back to the tenth century. In 946, Lady Trawst, wife to the Governor of Hawarden Castle, was praying before a large wooden statue of the Virgin Mary. She beseeched the statue to send down rain, there being a serious drought at the time. The image responded rather spitefully by falling on her, inflicting fatal injuries. Following this murderous assault, the statue was taken down in disgrace and thrown into the River Dee, whereupon it floated up to Chester on the incoming tide. The Cestrians treated it with reverence and buried it on the island, marking the spot with a stone cross.

The Roodee, being so close to the city, was a natural place for its citizens to take recreation, and it became the venue for such activities as archery, an annual (and extremely rough) Shrove Tuesday football match, foot races and horse racing.

In the 1970s and 1980s there were a number of reports about a massive black dog being seen loping menacingly around the Roodee. Large, dark, spectral beasts, especially hounds, crop up with some regularity in English folklore. Up and down the country every year hundreds of supposed sightings are reported to the police and the creature most often mentioned is a great black dog with glowing eyes and sometimes with phosphorescence around its jowls. These spectral hounds go by various names in different parts of the country (for example, the 'Black Shuck' in Norfolk and the 'Gurt Dog' in Somerset). In the north-west they are usually referred to as 'shrikers' but they are also sometimes called a 'barguest'. Their luminosity and evil appearance has led them to be associated with the Devil or his agents. They are said to react unhappily if they provoke hysterical reactions in those that see them but if they are simply accepted and left to their own devices, they are largely harmless. The Chester black dog seems to have been of a placid temperament, being glimpsed going around its business but fortunately not being chased or hounded… Perhaps this dog was just passing through, because there have been no more reports about it since.

After leaving the Stanley Palace, readers might like to take a walk along the city walls via Nuns Road and Castle Drive to Bridgegate. This walk provides excellent views across the Roodee and then of the picturesque Old Dee Bridge, which dates from the fourteenth century but was widened in the 1820s. In the street called Greyfriars which runs between Nuns Road and Nicholas Street, on the right and going towards the latter, there is an old house with prominent buttresses supporting the frontage, in the doorway of which a newspaper photographer once saw a mysterious wraith-like figure.

Nicholas Street provides very occasional sightings of a ghost coachman. Those who have seen him know he is a coachman because he proudly flaunts his livery, boots and tricorn hat in best coachman's

House in Greyfriars.

Bedroom in Recorder House.

fashion. What the ghost makes of the traffic which hurtles incessantly along this street, goodness only knows. How it must yearn for a return to an altogether slower, less dangerous but more graceful form of transportation.

Before reaching the Old Dee Bridge, readers will pass what is currently (2008) a building site close to the Grosvenor Bridge. In the Middle Ages the Benedictine nunnery of St Mary stood on this site. It was founded in the twelfth century and dissolved between 1537 and 1540. The site was later used for the town house of the Breretons. Sir William, a staunch supporter of Parliament, made himself so unpopular in the city during the Civil War that an angry mob descended on his house and demolished it. The site then went through a number of other uses. One of these was as a barracks for the local militia from the 1860s and, when that was demolished, as the location for the local police headquarters which opened in 1967. This fitted precisely the description 'concrete block', and besides having absolutely no architectural merit whatever, its uncompromising bulk and ugliness were particularly inappropriate in the sensitive surroundings of Chester and so close to the Castle. It has been demolished recently and the site is being redeveloped.

Excavations have revealed much of the plan of the nunnery and some of its fabric. One arch has been re-erected in Grosvenor Park. Before the old barracks were pulled down, indistinct but scary apparitions were seen around the buildings and especially looking from windows.

Just east of the Bridgegate high up on the city walls overlooking the weir on the Dee stands Recorder House. This is a small, comfortable and characterful hotel in which at least two guest bedrooms are reputed to be haunted. They are 'Libra' and 'Capricorn'. Those cleaning these particular rooms have sometimes felt that they were not entirely alone while doing their work, although they knew that they should have been. They sensed an indefinable although not threatening presence. Some while past two psychic investigators stayed in one of the rooms and experienced and recorded various phenomena which convinced them that the building was haunted.

Bear and Billet Inn

Just inside Bridgegate on the west side of Lower Bridge Street is the very picturesque and genuinely half-timbered Bear and Billet Inn. An older building preceded it on the same site and what can be seen today dates, with some restoration, from 1664 – which makes it rather late for a half-timbered town house. At one time it belonged to the very rich Talbot dynasty, the Earls of Shrewsbury, and it was their Chester residence. They had many and more grandiose houses elsewhere. Curiously the Bear and Billet was the insignia of the Earls of Warwick and is often known by its alternative name of the Bear and Ragged Staff. For many years the pub sported a sign showing a chained bear. It now (2008) displays a sign in a more contemporary and less heraldic idiom, attractive for all that.

The normal occupant of the house was the earl's bailiff whose job, among others, was to collect tolls on goods entering the city via the Old Dee Bridge close by. It was only to be expected that such a man would be disliked by virtue of his job but one of the bailiffs was truly loathsome. He systematically ill-treated his servant girl and on one occasion beat her and then locked her in one of the smallest rooms in the house. No sooner had he done this than he was called away on business. Off he went, forgetting the captive servant girl. The business took several days and it was only on his way back that he suddenly remembered what he had done. Arriving back at the house, he hurried to the room only to find that the girl had died, obviously slowly and agonisingly, of starvation. Occasional unexplained noises over the centuries have been attributed to her ghost.

Bear and Billet Inn.

Recently the building was given a very thorough renovation and workmen related many cases of inexplicable noises, sudden drops in temperature and a 'presence', invisible and intangible, but horribly menacing for all that. One of the men forgot his sandwiches and his partner brought them to the pub. She was accompanied by the family dog. Apparently the dog's hackles rose and his normally proud tail went into freefall as they approached the pub. When they arrived at the door the dog gave off the most mournful wailing noise and tugged feverishly on his lead in his determination to get away as quickly as possible.

Those who investigate supernatural phenomena argue that bursts of paranormal activity often follow renovation work in old buildings as if the disturbance of their fabric somehow also disturbs the spirits they contain, which then manifest themselves, perhaps after centuries – or at least years – of relative or absolute quiescence. In the case of the Bear and Billet, it would not be unreasonable to suppose that the phenomena experienced during the building works were produced by the spirit of the cruelly used servant girl. It would also not be unreasonable to suppose that, having had her uneasy repose disturbed by the knocks and bangs associated with the renovation works, this spirit emerged intent on wreaking vengeance on the callous bailiff.

There is nothing very alarming about the Bear and Billet's other ghost – unless, that is, the person who sees it is someone frightened by the whole idea of ghosts. It has frequently been seen and takes the form of a gentle and kindly-looking elderly lady who gives a welcoming smile to male customers on the stairs. Apparently female customers are studiously ignored. No explanation has been given for who the ghost is or for its rather blatant sexual discrimination.

St Mary's Hill

The steepest street in Chester, St Mary's Hill, runs between Lower Bridge Street and Castle Street. For many years St Mary's Hill claimed to be the steepest street in any English town or city. It is possible to think of other, more certain contenders for the title – Steep Hill in Lincoln would do for a start, but St Mary's Hill is now out of the race because traffic is banned and so now it is in effect a rather classy footpath.

St Mary's Hill is tucked away off the beaten track and ill-frequented, especially out of working hours. It can be extremely atmospheric and not a little spooky to walk up the cobbled part of the hill after dark on a misty winter's evening, with the floodlit tower of St Mary's-on-the-Hill visible above and a murky aura around the street lamps.

St Mary's Hill.

Shipgate Street.

At the bottom of St Mary's Hill in Shipgate Street people claim to have heard early in the morning the lowing of what sound like distressed cows. This may seem rather incongruous in such an urban location, but centuries ago a cow-keeper maintained a herd of dairy cows at this point. There was a ready market for their milk in the city. One night the cow-keeper passed away in his sleep and as the hours passed the woebegone creatures, hungry and desperately in need of being milked, set up a mournful mooing, the sound of which has come down to us over the ages.

The Old Rectory

Near the top of St Mary's Hill is the Old Rectory. A small room on the top floor is always icily and unwontedly cold. As if that is not enough, the door to this room is closed, even slammed, when there is no one there to do the slamming. There doesn't have to be any wind for this to occur. They found it hard to keep their staff in the building, which is now let out as offices.

A house in Castle Street is said to contain a poltergeist whose activity seriously scared an electrician doing some installation work but which is regarded with total nonchalance by the owner.

Exterior of Ye Olde Kings Head.

The sword and sandals in the Old Kings Head.

Ye Olde Kings Head

This handsome seventeenth-century building has a timber-framed top storey and a riot of fine ancient internal woodwork. It is said to stand on the site of the first stone-built house in Chester of which there is a record. No fewer than four men with the name Randle Holme made their mark in Chester between the 1550s and early 1700s. Of four consecutive generations, three were notable heralds and all were avid collectors of historical material about Chester. A plaque on the outside of Ye Olde Kings Head claims that the second Randle Holme, the best known of the four, who was born in 1627, lived there when it was a town house.

On New Year's Eve 1982, a female guest was asleep in one of the rooms upstairs when she suddenly woke up at two o' clock in the morning. Those who knew her did not consider her to be the fanciful type and so took her evidence very seriously. As she sat up, she was able to discern what she described as a 'man in black'. Although she could not see his face, he apparently examined her from a distance for what she estimated was up to a quarter of an hour but may actually have been much less. Remarkably, she did not scream or even call out, and the apparition eventually evaporated into nothingness. The woman said that she did not feel threatened in any way, and indeed felt a sense of calm repose while the spectre stood immovable close to the bottom of the bed. Clearly an extremely cool character, she spent the second night of her stay at Ye Olde Kings Head in the same room. It was bedroom number six.

The ghost of a child sometimes appears upstairs, having a particular fondness for bedroom number four. There is also thought to be a poltergeist which bursts into activity from time to time. In one bedroom it scrawls messages on a mirror. In another it rather irritatingly moves guests' items around. The cries of a baby are sometimes heard even when there is no baby around to make them.

In the 1930s renovation work was taking place in the pub when a rather fine sword was discovered under the floorboards of bedroom four. The sword is in a cabinet in a room on the first floor but no one knows anything about it. It shares the cabinet with two ancient sandals. Do these items have anything to do with the pub's spooky phenomena? Some years ago, they were removed and examined – after which this part of the pub was suffused by an overwhelming smell of manure.

Staff say that there are parts of the building in which they feel uneasy if they are by themselves, especially when it is dark outside.

Falcon Inn

Yet another ancient hostelry that has a story or two to tell, the Falcon stands on the site of a house of medieval origin which was completely rebuilt in 1626. It was the fairly modest town house of the Grosvenor family who went on to become the Dukes of Westminster, one of the richest dynasties in Great Britain, as indeed they still are. Their later massive mansion, Eaton Hall, stood just south of Chester at Eccleston, and their power and presence can still be seen in much of the city's nineteenth-century buildings.

In due course they abandoned this house which, incidentally, has an ancient crypt and formerly had a row running through the front of it. It went through a variety of other uses, was thoroughly restored in the mid-1880s but later fell on hard times to the extent that by the 1970s it was so derelict as to be a candidate for total demolition. Fortunately it was acquired by a brewery with an appreciation of heritage and it opened as a pub again in 1982.

The old Falcon Inn.

The Falcon houses a well-attested poltergeist. The story is that the family who once occupied the house had a young servant girl who they systematically insulted and mistreated. Eventually they literally threw her into the street, on the grounds that she was lazy and useless. She was friendless, penniless and homeless and no one would take her in. She died of neglect and starvation. It is hardly surprising that she resented the callous way in which she had been treated and so she returned as a poltergeist to wreak havoc and fear among those who had driven her to her death. She does so by breaking glasses and moving articles about, and had there not been a smoking ban, she might to this very day have thrown the odd ash tray across the room. Her anger against those who abused her so cruelly is understandable, but in all fairness is it right for her to wreak her revenge by taking it out on the present-day staff?

No. 40 Bridge Street

These premises, currently a hair salon, have a ghost affectionately known as 'George'. Reports suggest that although he is quite active for a ghost, he is of a pleasant disposition and those who work on the premises do not regard him as any kind of threat.

Essentials.

The Dewa Roman Experience.

Dewa Roman Experience

In Pierpoint Lane off the west side of Bridge Street is the Dewa Roman Experience. This provides an attempt to reconstruct the sights, sounds and smells of Roman Chester. One or two visitors have had value-added experience – of the sort they did not expect. Some, always women, have felt unseen hands round their necks – the spectre of the Chester Strangler perhaps?

Former Ye Olde Vaults aka 'Barlow's'

For many years licensed premises, this building was haunted by a cantankerous former landlord called George Barlow who could be heard mumbling and grumbling *sotto voce* about the way in which his pub had fallen on hard times. It is thought that this was the spirit of a landlord known throughout the city for the excellence of his hospitality and housekeeping. His was a hard act to follow and subsequent landlords, in spite of their best efforts, presided over a pub that had become a mere shadow of its former self. Perhaps staying in the place, investing it with his brooding presence and occasionally also doing little bits of mischief like moving things about and putting them back in the wrong place, was the way in which the disgruntled former landlord thought he could get his own back on those who followed him.

'Barlow's' is now a shop called 'Essentials' offering manicure and other services to those who are interested.

No. 12 Bridge Street

Just up from Barlow's at No. 12 Bridge Street were the premises most Cestrians will remember in recent years as housing 'Bookland'. This was a splendid location for a bookshop. The building itself is mid-seventeenth century and timber-framed but the premises have a stone-vaulted crypt. For centuries, this crypt had been bricked up and filled with rubble and it was only 'rediscovered' in the nineteenth century. A trio of late thirteenth-century windows can be seen at the rear of the shop.

It is said to be haunted by the apparition of a boy, described as looking like an apprentice and dressed in clothes of the Victorian period. According to the legend he slipped and fell on some stone steps at the back of the shop, receiving fatal injuries. He roams restlessly and perhaps resentfully around the crypt – no doubt in today's world he would be going to one of the insurance companies that specialize in personal injury and suing the shop for every penny he could get. On occasions he also manifests himself in an upstairs room.

No. 12 is now a shop called 'Cruise' selling shoes and other fashion items.

EERIE EVENTS IN
THE EAST

Tudor House

On the left, half way down Lower Bridge Street stands Tudor House. This is an early seventeenth-century building of which the two upper storeys are half-timbered and the lower two composed of brickwork. Close examination reveals that there was once a row at first-floor level, as indeed there was with several other of the older buildings in this street.

Three hauntings are reported from Tudor House. One is the apparition of a man without a head. This fits in well with the story that the figure observed from time to time belongs to a wealthy cavalier who was resident in Chester during the great siege of 1645 to 1646. By the worst of bad fortune, he happened to be gazing out of an upper casement window, perhaps breathing in the night air, when what was either a stray Parliamentary cannonball or an extremely well-aimed fluke neatly removed his head. Headless this spectre may be, but he does not allow that to deter him from dressing in the height of seventeenth century style and modishness. In fact, just about the only item he needs to complete his fashion statement is a broad-brimmed hat with feather decorations. Clearly he is a ghost who pays close attention to detail so far as his appearance is concerned, but obviously he has nowhere to hang his hat.

The other two hauntings consist of a fairly mundane grey lady, who paces restlessly around one of the landings, and an impatient spook which manifests itself by treading heavily and then rattling locks and belabouring doorknobs on the top floor.

Pepper Street Chapel

On the south side of Pepper Street is an old chapel with a neo-Classical front. This originally housed meetings of the Methodist New Connexion and was opened in 1835. It closed for the purposes of worship just after the First World War. The building found other uses and had various frontages which largely hid the chapel behind. In fact the chapel was only 'rediscovered' in 1984 during building work. In recent years it has housed branches of 'Habitat' and 'Multiyork'.

The Pepper Street Chapel provides a home for two of Chester's best-known ghosts. They go by the names of Charlie and Herbert. Although they had made their generally benevolent presence felt over several decades, they suddenly came to prominence in the 1960s. At that time the building was used as a

Tudor House.

garage and in order to give him a competitive edge over his rivals, the proprietor decided to try and see whether it was worth opening twenty-four hours a day. None of the existing staff was prepared to do the night shift so the owner had to advertise for someone specifically prepared to work nights. No sooner was the first recruit installed than he left, making a number of tart comments on his way out about his lonely vigil being disrupted by a couple of hooded monk-like figures who flitted in and out of the doors to the garage, irrespective of whether they were open or closed. He thought they had made their way up from the nearby river, but when they were anywhere near the petrol pumps, they simply vanished. Although they made no noise and did not seem threatening, understandably they gave the man the creeps.

Another advertisement was placed, another night-shift worker recruited. Charlie and Herbert put in their appearance – the new recruit left. This happened with almost monotonous regularity until the proprietor recruited his first female worker. She must have been made of sterner stuff, as she stayed for several weeks and happily admitted that she regularly saw what she described as a couple of monks but although they acted rather oddly, they gave her no cause for alarm. In fact at first she used to call out

Pepper Street Chapel.

cheerfully to them, but their response was either to vanish immediately or to pass through the door, irrespective of whether it was open or closed, into the garage building – whereupon they disappeared from sight. All this she took in her stride, although she thought they were a bit ill-mannered not to answer her greeting. She continued until the proprietor decided that he was not doing enough trade to make it worthwhile to pay somebody to fill the night shift. The girl took the termination of her employment every bit as phlegmatically as she took the regular appearance of Charlie and Herbert.

The building has gone through several other uses since then but there have been no reports of their reappearance. Does this mean they are still there but there is no one to see them?

Marlbororough Arms

In St John's Street stands the Marlbororough Arms, a small mock half-timbered town pub. In 1885 the pub's landlord went down to the cellar – where he cut his throat during a fit of particularly severe depression brought on by the infidelity of his wife. This unhappy event is said to be responsible for the ghostly sound

Plaque on Pepper Street Chapel.

which sometimes emanates from the cellar. It resembles a gurgling noise and is supposed to be a re-enactment of the sound the luckless landlord made as his lifeblood gushed out of his self-inflicted and fatal wound.

A hundred years later, in 1885, a sign-writer was employed to restore the pub sign and the name on the façade of the building. Breaking off for a moment, for some reason or other he made his way down to the cellar, only to re-emerge almost immediately, shaking with fear and ghastly white. Somebody or something had scared the daylights out of him down there. Eventually, however, he managed to re-climb his ladder and get back to work, but he was so shaken up that he spelt Marlborough as 'Marlbororough'. The name remains miss-spelt to this day. Cestrians wouldn't wish it any other way.

A recent licensee who claims psychic powers has said that he has heard a number of unexplained noises and voices and has been in touch with the spirit of the earlier landlord who died by his own hand. He described the spirit as quite friendly and by no means threatening.

The Amphitheatre

One of Chester's best-known ghosts is that of a legionary soldier seen pacing restlessly around between the ruined Roman amphitheatre and the foundations of the ancient tower which once stood close to the present Newgate. This amphitheatre (which is Chester's oldest known building and the biggest of its kind yet found in Britain) was discovered accidentally in 1929 during preliminary work for a new wing to be added to the Ursuline Convent School close by. About thirty years elapsed before systematic archaeological excavation began. Half the amphitheatre still remains hidden from view under later buildings and experts estimate that it had the capacity for an audience of 6,000.

The Malbororough Arms.

A good afternoon's entertainment which would have sent the audience home with the happy feeling that they had enjoyed good value for money would probably have consisted of half a dozen gigantic and muscular gladiators slowly fighting each other to painful and gory deaths. A supporting item in the programme might have consisted of slaves from one of Rome's many subservient nations – armed, if they were lucky, with a net – being stalked and pulled apart, or even better, visibly consumed, by hungry lions. There was nothing highbrow about popular culture in Roman Britain. A more permanent stone building replaced an earlier wooden amphitheatre around the end of the first century AD and these are the remains that can be seen today.

This ghost is by no means coy, having allowed itself to be seen over the years by dozens of witnesses. It is perhaps fortunate that among those who have clapped eyes on him, there are some who just happen to be experts in Roman military uniforms and they have averred with total certainty that he is a decurion of the Second Legion Adiutrix which is known to have been based at Chester around AD 70. A decurion was a kind of petty officer who commanded a troop of ten cavalrymen.

The poor chap died in very unhappy circumstances. He fell madly and passionately in love with a local Chester girl. It was a torrid affair – and unfortunately, the man in question allowed his rampant desire to

Roman amphitheatre.

affect his judgement. Such was his obsession with the girl that he abused his rank and thereby opened himself up to a justifiable charge of dereliction of duty. When things were quiet, he would tell his men to be vigilant and to attend assiduously to their duties while he blatantly neglected his own responsibilities. He used to nip out through a convenient nearby postern gate for a steamy tryst with his loved one. Unfortunately for him, as so often happened, the locals didn't like fraternisation with the Romans. This was entirely understandable because the Romans were, after all, part of an uninvited occupying army.

Our decurion's lust got the better of him once too often. He emerged from his love nest with a flush on his cheek and a spring in his step only to be set upon by a bunch of brawny local lads who clearly thought that he was overpaid, oversexed and over here. They grabbed him, gagged him and tied him up. The local men then sneaked through the unguarded postern, having rightly assumed that the Roman soldiers would be relaxing, confident in the knowledge that their leader was elsewhere and would be some time in returning. The decurion's assailants sublimated some of their pent-up resentment against the Romans by unleashing a savage attack on those they could find, killing several and injuring others, after which they scooped up as much booty as they could carry away. The decurion somehow managed to wriggle out of his bonds. Aware that he was in line for serious disciplinary proceedings in view of his wilful neglect of duty, he nevertheless realised that he would possibly make it even worse for himself if he didn't sound the alarm. Apparently he was on his way to do this when he encountered a straggler from the party of locals, who killed him on the spot.

No wonder his disembodied spirit still paces so restlessly and with such apparent emotional agitation in this part of the city. Is he reliving those moments of ecstasy that he enjoyed in the arms of his native *inamorata* and from which he was so suddenly and cruelly plucked away? Is he turning over in his mind and rehearsing the excuses for his presence elsewhere at such a crucial time which he would need to produce to defend himself against the charges his superiors would call him to answer?

The ghost of the decurion is seen in this vicinity, which is close to the south-eastern part of the city walls. There have always been those who, perhaps understandably, have enjoyed a hoax or spoof on the theme of ghosts and hauntings. In the late nineteenth century, stories began to spread about what became known as the 'Newgate Ghost'. It was a scary phantom which was often seen flitting around this part of the city walls, usually on moonlit nights. It put the wind up all those who saw it, but it did so once too often. It frightened one particular woman so much that she rushed home, visibly spooked and shaking with fear. She poured out her heart to her husband. Clearly he was the kind of man who acted first and thought afterwards, if indeed he thought at all. It was obviously dark but this mattered little as, with a lust for revenge burning inside him, he made straight for the city walls, determined to have it out with whatever or whoever it was that had so terrified his wife. The fact that he might be dealing with a ghost seems not to have mattered one iota. When he got to the walls, his luck was in. He spotted a shrouded figure, shouted various threatening obscenities and then gave chase. He caught up, and had to be prevented from beating seven bells out of the figure. The 'Newgate Ghost' turned out to be the wife of a prominent baker in the city. The police arrested her and the outcome was that she had to agree never to pull such a stunt again. Quite why she felt drawn to spend her spare moments haunting the city walls in such an unusual fashion has never been explained.

A curious legend surrounds the founding of St John's. In 689 Ethelred, the King of Mercia, travelled to Chester to visit his much-loved niece, the saintly St Werburgh, who was the Abbess of Chester. While he was in Chester, God told him to build a church at the spot where he found a white hart. Ethelred was a man of pious disposition and he hastened to obey God's instruction. White harts were never ten a penny, even in those days, and Ethelred was at his wit's end wondering where he could find one so that he could embark on the building of the church that God seemed to require with some urgency. He had just decided to organize a hunting party when a report came in that a white hart had very obligingly turned up on a cliff overlooking the Dee, only a stone's throw from the abbey. Breathing an understandable sigh of relief, Ethelred was so grateful to the hart that he spared its life and promptly buckled down to the building work. It is perhaps the existence of this story which has been responsible for a number of claimed sightings of a spectral white hart in the vicinity of the church. The legend is commemorated in a stained glass window in the porch.

St John's church became a cathedral in 1072. Work started on creating a building of the size and dignity expected of a cathedral but this was abandoned around 1095 when the bishop decided he preferred to carry out his duties from Lichfield and Coventry rather than Chester. When a new diocese of Chester was created in the 1530s during the Dissolution of the Monasteries, the Benedictine Abbey of St Werburgh's was chosen for the honour of being the cathedral of the new diocese. The cathedral was rededicated, this time to Christ and the Blessed Virgin Mary. St John's became a parish church and with the building being too large for that purpose, much of the east end was demolished or allowed to become ruinous. A look around the interior of the truncated building will give some idea of just how grand St John's might have been had it not fallen on hard times. During the siege of Chester in the Civil War, snipers used the tower of St John's as a place from which to take pot shots at anything they could see moving on or around the walls.

It is hardly surprising that such an ancient and historic building claims to be haunted. Visitors have seen a spectral nun flitting around the church. People have got close enough to her to describe her face as 'beautiful' and her clothing as blue. A rather gruesome mural memorial of 1693 to Diana Warburton

Stained-glass window in St John's church
showing Ethelred and the white hart.

has a skeleton grinning mirthlessly while holding a carved message extolling the lady's virtues. Such *memento mori* were once used to remind the living of the inevitability of their own death. Other memorials close by to Katherine Wynne (1635) and Cornelius Hignette (1785) also display related *memento mori*.

One ghost associated with St John's has only been manifesting itself for something like the last 130 years. On 14 April 1881 the tower of St John's collapsed without warning. No sooner had the dust settled than reports came in that the ghost of an Anglo-Saxon monk had started putting in an appearance in the neighbourhood. He had the disconcerting habit of vanishing as soon as witnesses tried to focus their eyes on him but some of those who claimed to have encountered him said that he spoke in what sounded like a Germanic tongue. Perhaps this was Anglo-Saxon. Others claim to have heard or seen him praying. Some cynics reckoned that the mysterious monk was simply a hoaxer who got his kicks from spooking people. Such things have been known.

Visible high up in the ruins at the east end of St John's church is a curious niche usually referred to as 'The Coffin in the Wall'. It contains what looks something like a coffin on which are inscribed the words 'Dust to Dust'. One story is that it was unearthed by the sexton of St John's while digging a grave. Another version is that it was placed there by a clergyman named Richardson in 1813, having been brought by canal from Nantwich. Either way, why was it placed there and what was its purpose?

Memento Mori in St John's church.

Interior of St John's.

The Coffin in the Wall at the ruined east end of St John's.

The Anchorite Cell

Was this mysterious monk-like ghost whose repose had apparently been disturbed by the collapse of the tower of St John's the same apparition which is occasionally espied drifting across the nearby bowling green to the curious little building known as the Anchorite Cell, the Rock House, the Ankers Chapel or the Hermitage? This is tucked away in the overgrown quarry just below St John's church and looks as if it is composed of stone from the ruinous parts of that building. It is now a private dwelling but was once used as a retreat for those monks who found the hurly-burly of monastic life too much. There they could recharge their batteries, so to speak, and commune with the Almighty in the quiet, serene surroundings.

The whole point about being a hermit is to abjure the material world and its works and to live an isolated, solitary and austere life in commune with God. This being so, why did the hermit occupying the Anchorite Cell or at least its predecessor on the same site around 1066 enjoy so many visits as well as a variety of creature comforts brought to him by a woman with whom he was clearly on very close terms? Every age and every place has its chattering classes and soon those in Chester were buzzing about the identity of the hermit and the woman who so faithfully saw to his needs. Rumours started to circulate that the woman was Queen Ealdgyth and the man none other than King Harold Godwinsson who had led the English against the Normans at the Battle of Hastings.

This is where the story becomes complicated. At one time every schoolboy knew that Harold copped it in the eye at the battle and that his death rather knocked the stuffing out of his tired and beleaguered followers. They fought on for some time but in the knowledge that victory for Duke William's forces was little more than a formality. That is what we were told. As so often happens where history is concerned, what really happened may have been somewhat different.

A close examination of the battle scene on the Bayeux Tapestry suggests that it was one of William's aides who took the arrow in the eye. Harold's death may have resulted from some of Duke William's cavalry breaking through to the English centre and cutting down their leaders, including Harold, and hacking them to death. In their blood-frenzy, the ferocious Normans then mutilated many of the English corpses. Care needs to be exercised in using the Bayeux Tapestry as a piece of historical evidence because it was designed as a piece of political propaganda.

The story goes that after the battle, the chastened English camp-followers moved among the dead attempting to identify them. Edith of the Swan-neck, who was Harold's long-standing mistress, in effect his common-law wife, eventually identified her lover's body by a mole on the left buttock or some such distinguishing mark and is supposed then to have spirited his body away for burial at Waltham Abbey in Hertfordshire. Another story is that Harold was injured but did not die and was secretly removed from the field of battle to Dover Castle. He was of course a fugitive and he decided to adopt the appearance and lifestyle of a hermit. This was probably a fairly good cover and using it, Harold eventually found suitable premises at Chester. There he was visited by his Queen – who is supposed to have previously sought sanctuary in Chester – and one or both of them were recognized. It was said that the hermit was half-blind. If there is any truth at all in this story, then it seems strange that the Normans were not informed. One would have expected them to move with their customary

The Anchorite's Cell.

efficiency and ruthlessness and take the appropriate measures. Legend says that Harold lived in the cell for about seven years and only revealed his true identity on the death bed.

This really is a farrago of historical confusion. However, there have been innumerable reports over the centuries of a ghost at the Anchorite Cell. Is it the ghost of Harold or is there some much simpler explanation?

There have long been rumours of a secret underground passage from the Anchorite Cell to St John's church. Stories of such tunnels abound all over Britain and romantic as they may sound, it is pointless to take them too seriously.

The monkish ghost sometimes seen around the area of St John's church and the Anchorite Cell is perhaps the same ghost who has been glimpsed in the narrow, somewhat gloomy alley between high walls that climbs up from up from The Groves towards the west end of St John's church. On one occasion he was seen after a snowfall but was so incorporeal that he made no footprints in the snow.

The Old Bishop's Palace

The Groves form a pleasant promenade along the side of the Dee and attract massive crowds on sunny high days and holidays. The Old Bishop's Palace can be seen up on the right when walking from Queen's Park Bridge towards the Old Dee Bridge. The palace possesses two supernatural phenomena. One is supposedly the ghost of a boy employed in the house to look after and clean the family's boots. For some peccadillo, this rather pathetic little wean was dismissed; thrown out into the snow of a bitter winter's day. Shortly after, his tiny body was found by the Dee. He had frozen to death. However, it seems that he

Old Bishop's Palace.

has managed at least partly to get his own back. Subsequent occupants of the house have been driven to distraction by the frequency with which items of footwear disappear, always at inconvenient times. Just when their owners have given up hope of ever seeing the missing shoes again and have gone out and bought replacements, the items mysteriously turn up once more. A variation is for boots and shoes simply to be moved around, turning up in places where they get in the way or create a hazard. Is this the work of the poltergeist of this poor maltreated servant?

Lest the bishop be accused of a marked lack of Christian compassion, it has to be said that he was absent from the palace when the boy was ejected so callously. He is supposed to have been a hard-working servant but somehow he managed to get on the wrong side of the housekeeper and it was she who dismissed him.

The other weird phenomenon is the occasional sound of a whip cracking in the old stable yard. This is generally thought to be the ghost of a former coachman who worked for the bishop. This man is supposed to have been a virtuoso with a whip. Those with suspicious minds might wonder exactly what this meant. However, in the twenty-first century there is no one there to crack a whip – indeed, there hasn't been a coachman or as much as an ostler about the place for generations.

This building was the Bishop's Palace from the 1870s to 1921 and it is now prestigious offices.

The Newgate

By the late 1920s the old Wolfe's Gate was proving to be an obstruction to the apparently inexorable growth of road traffic. The result was the Newgate, a wider opening in the city walls built in an interesting mixture of ancient and modern styles, completed in 1938.

Close by there lurks a kind of 'audio-ghost', one who is never seen but only heard. What is more is that it is only heard at night, although it is impossible to hear much at this spot anyway because of the motorised pandemonium of the inner ring road. The spectral sound takes the form of the insistent beat of galloping hooves.

The story behind this noisy phenomenon is that in Tudor times there was a youthful armourer called Luke who fell head-over-heels in love with a gorgeous young thing by the name of Ellen Aldersey. She was the daughter of Alderman Aldersey, a man with fingers in innumerable pies who considered himself and his daughter of infinitely higher social class than a mere armourer. Although Aldersey doted on his daughter, he considered that Luke was not good enough for her and he loftily forbade the proposed marriage of the two young people. For her part, Ellen could not contemplate the idea of life without her beloved. He, Luke that is, decided that he wasn't going to be pushed about by such an autocratic bigwig.

The couple concocted a plot. They decided to elope. Some while later Ellen was socializing with friends when she made some excuse and slipped away inconspicuously to the Pepper Gate where Luke was waiting equipped with two horses. They galloped off into the great blue yonder – actually it was Wales – to enjoy a life of marital bliss. The Alderman had steam coming out of his ears when a very scared servant told him what had happened. He was determined to make somebody bear the brunt of his rage and he turned on the gatekeepers. He berated them for not being vigilant enough to prevent the elopement. Having lost all reason, he then ordered them to keep the Pepper Gate permanently locked. This futile gesture gave rise to an ironic local saying, 'When the daughter is gone, lock the Pepper Gate.' This of course is Chester's very own version of the old proverb about closing the door after the horse has bolted. The episode was made the subject of a mock-medieval epic in poetry by the well-known Cheshire local poet Egerton Leigh.

The Newgate.

The story has a reasonably happy ending. Over the years the worthy Alderman Aldersey became reconciled to his daughter's choice and the couple were able to return to Chester several years later and enjoy a family reconciliation. The question that cannot be answered for certain is whether the ghostly hoof beats are those of Luke and Ellen's horses as they galloped pell-mell out of the city.

Ursuline Convent School

Off Little St John's Street stood the Ursuline Convent School in what was once known as Dee House. It is not used as a school now but many people who have worked in there in the past have agreed that it has an unpleasant and threatening atmosphere. It is claimed that an old woman wanders around the top floor and that she doesn't even have to appear but can exude a malevolent air which fills the entire building and accounts for the disenchantment of those who have had to work there.

Controversially, most of the premises have been boarded up and empty for some years and constitute (early 2008) something of an eyesore in this part of the city.

Ursuline Convent School.

Grosvenor Park

Grosvenor Park was created by the 2nd Marquess of Westminster in 1867 for the citizens and it adds much to this quarter of the city. It possesses a ghost who can only be described as 'overzealous'. He is known to all and sundry as 'Billy Hobby'. He is best described as a gadfly – a perishing minor nuisance because of his persistent habit of invisibly locking the park gates when they should be open and equally opening them up at times when the public is supposed to be excluded.

There was a Billy Hobby in real life and he was something of a scally. Among his jobs was that of looking after the spring of pure water that flowed to the surface in the park. To this day there is a curious little Gothic structure not far from the Dee known as Billy Hobby's Well. Always on the lookout for a spot of extra income he hit on the idea of charging people to have access to the water. He put about the idea that the spring had magical properties and included the shrewd marketing claim, which many found too persuasive to ignore or resist, that any unmarried woman who stepped into the small pool which collected on the surface on New Year's Eve would marry the first handsome man she met afterwards. As could have been confidently predicted, women queued up in droves on New Year's Eve and Billy made a small fortune by charging admission. This lucrative little scam paid its way on several consecutive New Year's Eves until two of his patrons caught a chill and died after standing around in the pool. The city fathers blamed Billy and he was forced to stop this particular little sideline. Doubtless he had others.

Is there a ghost story in here somewhere? Did Billy have the job of opening and closing the park gates as well as looking after the spring? If so, is it his spirit which returns from time to time and gets its own back winding up the park attendants by tinkering about with the gates? On the other hand, is there

Billy Hobby's Well.

some force of a more formidable nature at work in Grosvenor Park? There are those who claim that the name 'Billy Hobby' is an indication that it is no mere ghost that makes a nuisance of itself but a 'Hob' or 'Hobgoblin'. This is a kind of powerful mischievous spirit which humans do well to propitiate. Over the recorded history of humankind, there have been many occasions on which people have rued the day when they failed to treat them with the required degree of respect.

In the park and standing close to each other are three re-erected arches not *in situ*. They come from the Shipgate, the church of St Michael and (the one perhaps most likely to have brought supernatural phenomena with it) the Benedictine nunnery of St Mary.

W.H. Samuels, Eastgate

These premises were at one time a pub with the pleasing name of the Bear's Paw. It is now a jeweller's shop standing at the junction of Eastgate and Frodsham Street. Over the years, the staff working there have had reason to believe that they share their workplace with a fairly benevolent ghost called 'George'. Was he a regular from the days when it was still a pub who loved the place so much that he returned after death?

Arch in Grovesnor Park.

The Eastgate

The present arch of the Eastgate was erected in 1769. It is of course topped by one of the silliest clocks imaginable, one that would have been entirely at home in the cartoons by Emmet which graced the pages of *Punch* magazine between 1939 and 1958. Ridiculous or playful it may be, but it has become an icon of Chester and quite rightly, people have taken it to their hearts. The clock bears the date 1897 and was put up to celebrate Queen Victoria's Diamond Jubilee in that year. It actually started telling the time on 27 May 1899 (which marked Queen Victoria's eightieth birthday). Messrs Douglas and Mitchell designed the clock and its mechanism was by the eminent horologist James Joyce of Whitchurch.

A curious, somewhat sinister story is attached to the Eastgate. A Chester local paper reported that a married couple were doing their shopping on 30 August 1997 when they noticed three extremely unhappy looking old women close to the Eastgate. Instead of passing by not wanting to get involved, the wife approached them asking what the trouble was. One of them blurted out, between sobs, that the Princess of Wales had been killed in a car accident. Asked about when this had happened, the women made little response and moved away. When the couple got home, they switched on the radio and the television fully expecting them to be relaying information about the accident. Nothing. Later on that evening – in fact, ten full hours after they had seen the hysterical old women – the couple were watching

Eastgate clock at night.

a late-night movie when it was interrupted by the solemn announcement that the Princess of Wales had been seriously injured in a car crash in Paris. Who were the three mysterious old women and how did they know what they knew before the rest of the world knew it?

Thornton's Shop

How strange it is that Chester's most frequently sensed ghost is never actually seen!

The ghost is that of a girl and it is called 'Sarah'. She inhabits the shop on the north side of Eastgate Street currently occupied by Thornton's. Sarah's story is not an unfamiliar one. The girl probably lived in the eighteenth century and she was the victim of an unscrupulous young man who enjoyed her favours on the understanding that she and her lover would soon be married. This heartless young swain then jilted her, literally on the promised wedding day, so that he could continue his career of philandering with further maidens taken in by his honeyed words and charming ways. Sarah was so shocked and distressed that she retired to these premises in Eastgate Street, then in use as a house, and promptly committed suicide by hanging. After such a tragic and untimely death, it is perhaps not surprising that her spirit continues to manifest itself in and around the site of her suicide.

Thornton's shop, Eastgate.

This spirit manifests itself in just about every way that phantoms use to make their presence felt except the visual one. However, she makes up for that with another rare and remarkable attribute. This is the power of thought-transference, which in this case takes the form of putting into peoples' minds the words of well-known old songs. Everyone who has experienced the unaccountable way that a tune, often a very inconsequential one, may get into your head and then be very difficult to get out, will testify to just how infuriating this experience can be. The whole building is her domain but she seems to have a preference for the front room on the top floor and the cellar.

It does not do to mock Sarah. An American tourist who pooh-poohed the idea of the premises being haunted was knocked down the stairs by the hand of an unseen assailant. Severely chastened by the experience, she was prepared to make a legal declaration to the effect that she had received a very forceful but invisible blow between the shoulder blades. She went away actively revising her opinions about the supernatural. A meter-reader who casually descended to the cellar to do his job came back up the stairs with almost indecent haste and in a state of great agitation declaiming that he was never going down there again. When questioned, he blurted out that something or somebody with evil and malign intent had been waiting down there for him.

The rumoured presence on the premises of a haunting may even be good for business. Sarah is well-known and there may be people who pop in and make a purchase simply out of curiosity and to be able to say that they bought sweets in a haunted shop.

Sarah may not be a burglar alarm herself but she certainly alarmed one burglar! An intruder broke into the premises and managed to break into the safe. Although he went off with the day's takings, something must have disturbed and frightened him sufficiently for him to drop his tools and rush off. The investigating police officers were able to recover a full set of burglar's tools and a prime set of fingerprints. Doubtless he was soon busily helping the police with their enquiries.

Clearly Sarah remains deeply and justifiably embittered by memories of her perfidious paramour. She therefore seems to take singular exception to so-called tokens of romance and everlasting love as the various chocolaty concoctions decorated with red ribbons that are placed on sale annually around St Valentine's Day. She vents her spleen on these, scattering window displays in all directions and hurling boxes from the shelves to the floor. Attempts to exorcise Sarah do not seem to have been successful.

This well-documented activity has interested psychic investigators who have subjected the premises to various tests. They have concluded that Sarah is not alone! In fact, there seem to be two other paranormal presences: one seems to be a jovial tubby little fellow in an apron, and the other is described as 'an industrious man'. They say that two's company and three's a crowd, but this trio of spooky presences seem to rub along together happily enough.

The Thornton's shop is a regular stopping and talking point on city ghost walks. It is said that on at least one occasion the guide has been talking to the group with his back to the window while objects have been flying off shelves and across the shop with no signs of visible agency.

Boot Inn

The Boot Inn, which occupies a site in Eastgate Row North, is a small timbered pub of considerable charm and character – just the kind of ancient place that could reasonably be expected to house a ghost. Respectable now, in earlier times it was a bawdy house, in fact Chester's most notorious brothel. It is supposed to have been a place where Royalist troops caroused while off duty during the siege of the 1640s. At the rear of the building there were some wooden booths. These could be curtained off and were ostensibly used when men engaged in horse-trading wished to do business away from prying eyes and ears. Legend has it that these booths were appropriated by 'ladies of the night' who found the curtains came in useful when they carried out their own rather different business activities.

There are no apparitions at the Boot but sporadic reports have been made of ghostly noises very appropriate to the business formerly carried on there. These sounds, which emanate from the area where these booths were situated, include the convivial sound of the clinking of glasses. The more interesting ones, however, are apparently all definitely made by females and they include squeals of anguished delight, ecstatic groans and happy sighs of deep satisfaction. These present-day manifestations of the city's past should make living Cestrians ruminate happily on this evidence of the pleasures enjoyed by their ancestors.

St Werburgh Street

St Werburgh Street joins Eastgate Street and Northgate Street. In the vicinity of the spot where it makes a sharp left turn almost opposite the south transept of the cathedral, many witnesses have over the years reported one or more rather indistinct spectres. As far as can be described, they are dressed in military costumes of the seventeenth century. It is assumed that it or they are something to do with a vicious little skirmish that took place at this point in 1645 immediately after the Battle of Rowton Moor.

In the summer of 1645 things were not going well for Charles I and his cause. He spent the month mostly around the Welsh border and he was at Hereford when he heard that his supporter, the Marquess of Montrose, had just taken Glasgow. This welcome news may have caused the King to decide to join up with his Scottish supporters by proceeding via Chester, Lancashire and Cumberland to Scotland. He heard that Chester, a town which was one of his staunchest supporters, was seriously threatened by a powerful Parliamentary army. For their part, the soldiers and citizens of Chester took some heart from the knowledge that the King was about to join them.

This is not the place for a detailed account of the battle of Rowton Moor. Suffice it to say that although it was not a major battle, it was a serious setback for Charles, whose losses meant that he was unable to contemplate the march northwards to Scotland and was forced even more on the defensive. His soldiers were outnumbered and their morale was low, probably even before the battle had started and even more so when it turned into a rout. Many tired, wounded and scared Royalists made their way back into the city, mostly through the Northgate. The Eastgate had been blocked by many wagonloads of dung which the people inside the gates, now of course thinking defensively, hoped would act as a deterrent to the Parliamentary forces.

Eventually the Eastgate was breached by a jubilant Parliamentary force whose blood was up and who were intent on turning the one-sided slaughter into an absolute massacre. They charged along what is now Eastgate Street, turned into St Werburgh Street and approached the cathedral – only to run into a substantial body of Royalists. These men for their part had heard that the Eastgate had been breached and they were determined to strengthen the defences at that point. Space was very restricted and the confrontation turned into a bloody and confused hand-to-hand melee with quarter neither given nor expected. It is understandable that those who have seen something spectral assume that it is a psychic distillation of the powerful emotions released in this vicious and bloody struggle.

After a difficult and determined effort, the city gates were all made as secure as it was possible in the circumstances and presumably any Parliamentary troops still inside the walls were peremptorily put to the sword. For their part, the Parliamentarians withdrew some distance and started to dig in for a siege. They realised that Chester would be a tough nut to crack because of its powerful defences. For that reason it was necessary to box clever. They knew that psychology has a major role to play in warfare. Were there any methods that they could use to undermine the morale of the Cestrian defenders without putting themselves at risk through the use of force?

Major-General Poyntz hit on a clever ruse. It is said, which implies some doubt on whether this actually happened, that he ordered the decapitation of the hundreds of Royalist corpses which lay scattered around the bloody environs of Rowton Moor. He then ordered these heads to be thrown into the River Dee upstream from Chester. The idea was that they would then float down the river past Chester providing a grisly visible deterrent to a continued defiance of the Parliamentary forces outside the city. Who knows, citizens watching this gory flotsam and jetsam coursing past might even recognize friends, relations and neighbours. Even if this story is apocryphal, it has not prevented occasional reports of spectral severed heads with fixed, glazed expressions floating down the river. It has not been revealed how they negotiate the weir near the Old Dee Bridge.

Chester Cathedral

For all that this ancient, albeit heavily restored, building dominates central Chester, it features little in the accounts of hauntings in what is otherwise a city with more than its fair share of supernatural phenomena. Perhaps the nearest thing is an item from 1906 which records the replacement of a paving stone in the cloisters. This was removed because someone who was superstitious thought it bore the mark of 'the devil's footprint'. The next day the stone which replaced it bore the same mark.

Before it became a cathedral, this building was an abbey, a large and rich one at that. It was dedicated to St Werburgh. She is supposed to have died around the year 700. She was a saintly, gifted and powerful woman and various relics associated with her were brought to Chester in the late ninth or early tenth century. Her shrine became an object of great veneration and attracted pilgrims in huge numbers who were persuaded to part with large amounts of money in order to demonstrate their devotion to the sacred relics associated with St Werburgh. The shrine was destroyed in the 1530s but was eventually rebuilt and is one of the best examples in Britain of what a great medieval shrine must have looked like.

The most famous legend surrounding the saintly Werburgh concerns the time when, as a young woman, she came across a flock of geese who were ruining the economy of a particular village by eating all the corn that the peasants depended on for their livelihood. Werburgh was not the kind of woman to put up with this and she called the birds together and proceeded to give them an almighty rollicking about the sin of greed. Chastened, the geese slunk off and agreed to be on their way the next morning. However, during the night some poachers seized, killed, cooked and ate one of the geese. St Werburgh was incensed and then performed the miracle which led to her name being so revered. Punishing the poachers, she then restored the goose to life whereupon it rejoined its fellows and waddled off contentedly with them to pastures new. A misericord in the choir shows St Werburgh performing the miracle of raising the goose from the dead.

Night-time view of the cathedral from the south-east.

St Werburgh's shrine in the cathedral.

Abbey Green from the city walls.

Such stories are delightful even if it is hard to gives them the slightest credence. This has not, however, stood in the way of people coming forward occasionally to say that they have been in the environs of the cathedral at night and have heard the sound of geese when they know there are no geese in Chester city centre. The fact that the miracle of the geese is said to have occurred many miles from Chester provides no obstacle to those determined to believe that they have had a supernatural experience.

Abbey Green

One of the fine Georgian houses on Abbey Green, off Northgate Street, has been the centre of regular poltergeist activity. All sorts of items from the very lightest up to and including a solid cast-iron stove are moved around by what is obviously an extremely strong but invisible force.

The Phoenix Tower

The Phoenix Tower – otherwise known as King Charles's Tower – stands at the north-east corner of the city walls. The name 'Phoenix' comes from the emblem of the Painters' and Stationers' Co. who once used the building for their meetings. On the outside wall a damaged tablet displays a phoenix and the date 1613.

Chester was a base of great importance to the Royalist cause in the Civil War and was staunchly holding out for the King at a time when things were going very badly for his cause. For that reason he had decided to visit the city in 1645 with the intention of giving its beleaguered citizens a much needed morale-booster. The alternative name for this building recalls the fact that King Charles almost certainly made use of it in September 1645. He is likely to have found its height useful while making a preliminary survey of the area to the east and south-east of the city. He is likely to have done this survey while preparing for the possibly crucial battle with the Parliamentary army under Major-General Povyntz that seemed almost inevitable. This did indeed take place shortly afterwards at the Battle of Rowton Moor. The other explanation is that he used it to try to get some idea of how the battle was proceeding once it had started. In doing this, Charles was of course by no means the first – nor would he prove to be the last – monarch or politician who carefully remained in a place of safety while his troops fought and risked their lives on his behalf. At least the soldiers would have been assured that they had God on their side and that if they were wounded, maimed or slaughtered, their efforts, and even their ultimate sacrifice, would have helped to make the world a better place.

It has been pointed out that the King was unlikely to have got much idea of the battle from such a height and at such a distance although he may have gained some idea of how it was going when he saw injured Royalists making their way back to the haven of the city walls and perhaps in some cases being pursued by jubilant Roundheads. Perhaps because the view was not a good one, he probably then climbed the cathedral tower which was higher. When he was there, it seems that someone took a pot shot at him and it only narrowly missed the royal head. Who was the mysterious would-be assassin? Or was it a genuine stray bullet? Was it friendly fire? Over the years there have been sporadic reports that King Charles, in the form of a ghost, has been seen in his tower once more and also that the portion of the walls from the Eastgate to the Phoenix Tower sometimes resounds to the noise of artillery and musketry, the clang of swords and the manic cries of men fired by fury and fear.

King Charles's or the Phoenix Tower.

Kaleyard's Gate

On the eastern wall of the Abbey Green is Kaleyard's Gate, which was used by the brethren of the abbey to gain access to their vegetable garden. Incised on the wall close by are the enigmatic words '692ft' and an anchor. These were the work of a master mason by the name of William Haswell, and his companion, Musgrave, who owned a timber-yard. They were so impressed by the launching of the *Great Eastern* in 1859 that they felt constrained to commemorate the event in this way. This ship, by some way the largest ever built at that time, was 692ft long and was the ultimate achievement of Isambard Kingdom Brunel.

As far as is known, no supernatural phenomena have shown themselves in the specific vicinity of this gate but the carved hieroglyphs make reference to a 'jinxed' ship whose extraordinary run of ill-luck certainly has much of the paranormal about it. Four workers were killed while the ship was being constructed. A riveter and his apprentice disappeared and their mates reckoned that they had been accidentally sealed up in the ship's double-skin hull, their impassioned appeals for help being drowned by the din of the riveting guns. While undergoing sea-going trials a massive explosion seriously damaged the ship and caused injuries and death. Just before her maiden voyage, the captain, the coxswain and the young son of the purser were drowned when a sudden storm capsized their gig as they were rowing towards the shore.

The Kaleyard Gate.

This ill-luck meant that the *Great Eastern's* maiden voyage was completed with only thirty-five paying passengers. The crew numbered 418. The company made a thumping loss and insult was added to injury when a screw-shaft failed on the return journey and the ship could only limp along at reduced speed. When she reached Milford Haven, she fouled the hawser of a small boat and capsized it, drowning two of its occupants. She then managed to collide with a naval frigate. The *Great Eastern* never sailed to Australia, the task for which she had been designed. She experienced various other contretemps and became in effect something of a white elephant. When she was broken up, the skeletons of the riveter and his apprentice were found inside the double hull. Few mariners doubted that this grisly unofficial cargo was the reason for the ship's misfortunes.

SUBURBAN SPECTRES

We tend to associate suburbs with the rise of population, urban growth, the coming of the railways, of trams, buses and cars and also increased living standards and expectations from the eighteenth and nineteenth centuries onwards. However, Chester was by no means alone among walled English towns and cities in experiencing human settlement and building outside the protection of the town walls from as early as medieval times. Although the word 'suburb' may not actually have been in use, that is what such developments represent.

The idea probably most likely to come to our minds when the word 'suburban' is mentioned is an image of apparently typical serried ranks of rather smug 1930s-type semi-detached houses in streets often graced with pseudo-rustic names such as 'Acacia Avenue' and 'Laburnum Grove'. Obviously this concept contains a satirical element, but it brings out a sense of what is seen as the essentially mundane and commonplace nature of life in suburbia. Such roads – and often entire districts – can of course be found on the periphery of almost every town and city of any size in this fair land, and this includes Chester.

Suburbia on the face of it is unpromising territory for paranormal phenomena. This might seem to apply especially in the case of Chester given what seems to be the superfluity of ghosts in its central districts. However, in this section we will make mention of a number of reports of supernatural happenings from 'Chester beyond the walls'. They may not always bear comparison with the rich seam afforded by central Chester but one or two of them can certainly hold their heads up in the company of the most distinguished supernatural phenomena elsewhere.

In an upstairs flat in Blacon in 2005, the occupant was alone when he found himself unwittingly being used as a medium through which three deceased ex-members of the SAS tried to get in touch with a friend who was still alive. First he saw a tall figure of about 6ft 4in and aged in its late twenties. Clean shaven and with noticeably dark eyes, the figure was in full SAS uniform. That figure disappeared, to be replaced later the same evening by a very different apparition. This was aged in its sixties, had white hair and a noticeable pot belly and was in the uniform of an SAS regimental sergeant major. He was only about 5ft 4in but the superb polish on his boots was very evident. No sooner had he slipped from view than he was replaced by a younger-looking figure which was slightly taller. It had a face which was notably pock-marked.

The first figure reappeared briefly in the bedroom a few hours later. The occupant of the flat had a friend who had been in the SAS and he told him of his weird experience, perhaps expecting to have his leg pulled. On the contrary, the friend listened with rapt attention and told him that he recognised all three by their description. The two younger ones had died in action while the RSM had passed away of natural causes. He was sure that they were trying to get in touch with him to let him know that he was not forgotten and to remind him of the times they had shared. Presumably they chose the occupant of the flat because he was susceptible to messages from beyond the grave. He admitted that the experience did not scare him in the slightest and that he actually felt a great sense of peace when the apparitions made their presence felt.

To the north of the city in Liverpool Road stands a building erected in 1829 which in apparently less solicitous times was known rather bluntly as the County Lunatic Asylum. More recently it has been called the West Cheshire Hospital. In recent years, people working in what are now health authority offices on the site have reported a number of unexplained and unwelcome happenings. These have punctuated the working day but far from providing a welcome relief to the tedium of their normal routine, they have filled them with a dread of being alone when on the premises. A woman in black is sometimes seen, albeit indistinctly. Is she the figure who used to appear on the wards back in the nineteenth century when a patient was about to die?

The former Cow Lane is now called Frodsham Street and at its outer end it crosses the Shropshire Union Canal. On the south side of the canal and indeed making use of it for transport purposes was Griffith's flour mill. What has been described as 'ghostly' smoke has been seen in the vicinity. Some people have no truck with such fanciful notions and have put this phenomenon down to mist rising from the canal under certain weather conditions. In 1919 a drowned body was recovered from the canal at this point. Is this anything to do with the rather blurred-looking figure that some have claimed to see emerging from the canal itself and staggering uncertainly along the towpath? The figure has even been accused of lunging at passers-by, but as so often happens, all such reports without any substantiating evidence need to be taken with a pinch of salt. The mill itself dated from the early nineteenth century and was badly damaged by fire in 1975.

Brook Street which runs parallel to Hoole Way is now a rather run-down part of the city. The Top Rank bingo hall boasts of a ghost known as 'Old George'. Is he responsible for the unexplained bangs, dull thumps and crashes that emanate on occasions from the attic? Equally, is Old George the man dressed in a tweed jacket who appears on the balcony but makes himself scarce with disconcerting speed if approached or even hailed?

St Anne's Street is on the edge of the district of Newtown which was developed in the middle of the nineteenth century. Streets of terraces for working-class people gave the district the look of a northern industrial town. Indeed the dwellings in this area were mostly occupied by families having one or more members working close by, particularly on the railway. What eventually became the Great Western Railway Co., the London & North Western Railway and the Cheshire Lines Committee both had extensive installations in the vicinity.

In the late nineteenth century, an ordinary terraced house on St Anne's Street was the scenario for terrifying and inexplicable phenomena. A family with young children moved in and no sooner were they installed in the house than they had to endure frightening and sleepless nights. Time and time again footsteps were heard climbing the stairs and approaching their bedroom door, whereupon the sound abruptly ended. On the first night this happened, one child, bolder than the rest, got out of bed and flung open the door. Nothing there. Night after night the footsteps went through the same routine and the children grew accustomed enough to them simply to snuggle as far down the bed as they could, fairly certain in the knowledge that once the sounds stopped they would be able to get back to sleep.

Worse was to follow. The mysterious footsteps had been manifesting themselves for several weeks and the occupants of the house had become almost blasé about them. Then one night the family was sitting around the fire in the living room when, with a sudden and alarming rumble, several books came down

The canal basin.

the chimney, fell on the fire and were soon ablaze. Every member of the family was badly shaken by this unexpected cascade but the books were so quickly consumed in the flames that they were unable to ascertain what kind of books they were. The good news was that the scary footsteps ceased with immediate effect. To this day, no one has been able to provide a plausible explanation.

The hospitals of Chester have something of a reputation for being haunted. The Old City Hospital in the Hoole district made the headlines in 1976 when several of the nursing staff reported that they had seen what they described as a 'man in a brown suit' visiting an elderly woman patient. When they asked her later who her visitor had been, she denied having had one. They assured her that she had and described the person they had seen. The woman replied that the only person she knew that filled that description was her son and he had been killed in action in the Second World War.

A nurse who worked in the hospital in the 1970s related how on the night shift, she experienced lights going on and off mysteriously and seeing the shadowy figures of women, the most familiar of whom was a lady in grey. Curiously the nurse never felt scared by these apparitions but realised that what she saw was not seen by her colleagues. The hospital was a workhouse at one time.

Dee Hill's Park off The Bars contains a number of sumptuous villas in a little haven, the presence of which is probably unsuspected even by many who have lived in Cheshire all their lives. At No. 14 there have been reports of a spectral monk whose activities have disturbed those trying to get a good night's rest.

In an unspecified street in Boughton it is said that an old woman came out of a cupboard, kissed two boys asleep in bed and then vanished. This poses the question of 'how does anyone know?' Was there someone else in the bedroom who witnessed this rather odd behaviour? How many times did it happen? Doubtless if the same thing occurred today someone would try to arrest the lurker in the cupboard for being a paedophile.

The haunted bingo hall.

Dee Hill's Park.

The former leadworks stood on the north side of the Shropshire Union Canal. The tall shot tower remains a prominent feature of Chester's skyline and a rare surviving example of this highly specialized kind of industrial building. The leadworks had their ghosts. While the works were still in use, two security guards once saw a strange-looking old woman carrying a large bag. Curious as to what she was up to, they challenged her – whereupon she simply vanished. When the security guards described the figure they had seen, men who had been employed at the works for many years recognized her as 'Mrs Cox'. She had been a familiar sight in the neighbourhood for many years.

When the works were being demolished, the figure of a man dressed in blue overalls was seen on several occasions although he was not one of the demolition gang. It was thought that it was possibly the ghost of a drunkard who had been run down and killed by a train on the railway line close by. It is not unknown, however, for a ghost which has been inactive to make its first appearance ever or at least for a long time when its surroundings are disturbed by something like demolition. Understandably they are upset by this threat to their normal routine. Perhaps they manifest themselves in the hope of scaring away what they think is the threat or its human agents. The actual demolition of the building they have occupied can sometimes apparently bring about a total end to their activities. On other occasions, the ghosts move into premises close by or, with what seems like total nonchalance, resume their activities in the new building erected on the site of the old.

Boughton Heath has been plagued by a phantom jaywalker who made a habit of appearing from nowhere, running across the road in front of fast-moving vehicles and then vanishing before shaken and angry motorists have a chance to remonstrate with him.

At the Brown Heath crossroads in Christleton two shadowy figures sporting natty clothes of the Civil War period have been seen from time to time. This is perhaps not surprising since it is close to where the Battle of Rowton Heath was fought in 1645. The rather dispersed area over which the fighting took place is not a particularly rewarding one for those who like to visit and study battlefields. In fact action took place in the Waverton, Rowton Moor, Vicars Cross and Hoole Heath areas. From all of these there have been occasional reports of sightings of soldiers in Civil War garb and also of such sounds as the whinnying of frightened horses, the sound of muskets being fired, the clash of steel on cold steel and screams of pain and terror as if those who took part in it are re-enacting the battle.

The Old Dee Bridge was for centuries the lowest bridging point on the River Dee. An earlier timber bridge had been replaced by a stone one, probably in the late fourteenth century. Various modifications were made over the years and the bridge had been widened in 1826 (by which time it was becoming increasingly unable to handle the build-up of traffic). It was therefore a great relief when the Grosvenor Bridge was opened in 1833. One unexplained supernatural experience occurred as late as 1986. In that year a woman from the Handbridge district on the south side of the river was walking across the bridge when a neighbour spoke to her and promptly vanished before the stunned woman could summon up a verbal response. Her confusion was understandable. The neighbour had died some time previously! It was her ghost on the bridge.

Curzon Park is on the south side of the River Dee high up overlooking the Roodee and it contains many swanky villas which were part of a speculative development built in the 1850s when Chester was booming and was successfully attracting wealthy middle-class people to take up residence in and around the city. The serenity of its exclusive surroundings has been rudely disturbed from time to time by reports of the passionate sobbing of a spectral woman wearing Elizabethan clothes who stands under a (real) tree from which an equally spectral hanged man is suspended. It is claimed that this unnerving vision was seen on three consecutive nights by the witness. Most people would have changed the route by which they walked home.

Saltney is a westward extension of Chester and is just across the border into Wales. An unnamed but ordinary 1930s detached house in a street which you wouldn't give a second glance to has provided the scenario for a host of uncanny events. The occupant had a much-loved dog for many, many years. When it eventually died, it seems that it neglected to also leave the house – it has been glimpsed fleetingly since then but it leaves more tangible evidence that it is still around in the form of its unmistakeable hairs. The owner has had other dogs since and they have found certain parts of the house terrifying – they have howled at something they have seen or sensed and been so frightened as occasionally to have made a mess on the carpet. The owner believes that these dogs are in touch with their predecessor. The cat also acts as if it is seeing something invisible to human eyes.

A human 'presence' is frequently sensed which the occupier thinks is possibly her mother who passed away in the house many years ago. This manifests itself irregularly at any time of day or night – even on the kind of bright, sunny days when one hardly expects supernatural activity. Those in the house who have experienced something say it is not in the least threatening and they just take it as something which goes with the house. When the old lady died, she was found by the man of the house, lying on the floor. He had just put his four-year-old daughter to bed and she had no idea what was going on, yet the next day, when she was told, she was able to give a completely accurate description of what her 'Nan' had been wearing when she was found, despite the fact that that she had not seen the old lady that evening.

Mysterious shadows are often seen when there is no one there to make them and 'muffled' shouts are often heard, a door into the attic opens time and time again when nobody has been anywhere near it and doors open for no apparent reason and certainly without human agency. On occasion, orbs of

Old Dee bridge from the city walls.

View over the Roodee to Curzon Park.

floating light have been seen. Things are moved about by an invisible force. They are usually taken from their normal place and rather irritatingly put somewhere totally inappropriate. They are, however, never hidden. On one occasion a heavy gilt mirror fell off the wall without warning. How and why did it fall? The strong twine with which it was attached to the picture hook was intact and the hook had not come off the wall.

Saltney Ferry station closed on 30 April 1962. It stood on the main line to Holyhead close to its junction with the branch line to Mold and Denbigh and it was three and a half miles by rail from Chester General Station. A substantial settlement was built in the vicinity for railway workers and their families. Railways until their modernization from the 1960s were highly labour intensive and the Saltney district had an engine shed and busy freight marshalling yards. There were several reports that an old man was seen – but more often heard – pedalling around the area on a rusty bicycle with a notable squeak and a spookily flickering lamp. He did this in the witching hours after midnight but there would have been railwaymen going to and from work on shifts involving anti-social hours. He was widely said to be the ghost of a man who had hanged himself in one of the railway buildings of Saltney.

CHESTER'S HAUNTED HINTERLAND

Backford

Backford is a small settlement on the A41 road about four miles north of Chester. Backford Hall was built in 1863 and is a brick building of vaguely Elizabethan style. It looks older than it is and forms the core of a complex of buildings used by Cheshire County Council.

In 1979 a female employee of the council was standing outside her own building at around 7.30 a.m. Looking up at the Old Hall, she was surprised to see what she thought was the face of an old lady looking at her, an old lady with a sad face. She looked away for a second and when she looked again the old lady's face had vanished from the window. The experience puzzled her and, later in the day, she walked past the same window and noticed a large desk fan where the face had been. Her curiosity aroused, the next day she asked one of her colleagues who worked in the Old Hall who would have been in that particular room the previous morning. She was told that the room would have been empty at such an early hour.

Clearly puzzled by what she thought she had seen, she spoke to one of the caretakers a few weeks later. He was not particularly surprised, rather nonchalantly telling her that she must have seen one of the ghosts of Backford Hall. Expanding on the theme, he then told there were supposedly no fewer than three ghosts that haunted the Old Hall. One, he assured her, was indeed an old lady. The other two were an old man and a young girl, the latter having fallen down the stairs to her death. He added that there was an attic room in the Hall that some of the staff refused to go into because of its scary atmosphere and the stories that were told about it being haunted.

Beeston

Beeston is a small and scattered settlement several miles out of Chester in a south-easterly direction. It is well known for its spectacularly sited ruined castle on a cliff 740ft high. It was built around 1220 to guard the approach to Chester. Even today, in its ruined state, it dominates its surroundings with quite extraordinary panache.

An enduring legend is that of King Richard III's treasure. Knowing that some of his staunchest supporters came from Cheshire, he is said to have felt reassured when, in 1485, he left literally a King's ransom in treasure at the castle before he rode off to meet his end at the Battle of Bosworth in 1485.

His supporters decided to hide it when news came of Richard's defeat and death, and are said to have done so in a shaft 370ft deep. Many attempts have been made to recover the treasure, but always without success. Some of those who have tried to do so have had inexplicable accidents soon afterwards and there is a rumour that the treasure is guarded by a ghostly presence that wreaks its revenge on those who get too close to the tantalising but apparently unreachable hoard.

Bunbury

An attractive village south-east of Chester, the winding lanes in the locality are supposedly haunted by a large white hound loping along and dragging a length of chain behind it. Also apparently seen from time to time is a ghostly horse and rider which dashes unexpectedly across the lane at breakneck speed. Both of these phenomena manifest themselves at dusk.

Duddon

Duddon is a small village on the A51 a few miles east-south-east of Chester. It has a pub with the possibly unique name of the Headless Woman. According to tradition, it gained this name because of an unpleasant incident during the English Civil War of the 1640s. The local squire, Joseph Hockenhull, was an ardent Royalist and had reason to believe that a Parliamentary patrol was on its way to arrest him. Therefore he hid all his valuables and went into hiding with his family and servants. He left just one servant, a housekeeper, Grace Trigg, in charge of the family home, Hockenhull Hall. He thought that the soldiers would not harm her.

He was wrong. The soldiers were pretty sure that Hockenhull had stashed his valuables away somewhere and so they set to work ransacking the house but without success. Getting angrier by the minute they then tortured Grace – who staunchly refused to reveal the whereabouts of the family silver. Finally, at their wit's end, the soldiers lost patience and cut off her head. One account says that for some unknown reason the soldiers put her body and severed head in a sack and dragged it to some cottages on the site of which the pub now stands.

The sudden, cruel and undeserved demise of Grace appears to have created such an outburst of psychic energy that, it seems, her spirit refuses to lie down. This is perhaps hardly surprising given that she was clearly a woman of great courage. What is thought to be her ghost is seen from time to time. At least, a woman apparently carrying her head under her arm is seen, and what would be more natural than to assume it is Grace? She walks lanes and field-paths, usually those that lead to the pub. She also puts in occasional appearances at the hall.

The pub itself has over the years witnessed innumerable unexplained noises, sudden feelings of iciness and the jostling of invisible elbows. These phenomena attracted psychic investigators who concluded that the Headless Woman is perhaps home to no fewer than six ghosts. Five of these died in the seventeenth century while the sixth was a man unfortunate enough to have suffered a fatal heart attack in 1943.

The pub's name therefore reflects this rather horrible piece of Civil War history, but it may not in fact be a direct reference to Grace Trigg. Although this is possibly the only Headless Woman pub, there are a number with names like the Silent Woman, Quiet Woman or Good Woman. They usually depict a woman without a head – and for that reason they are definitely politically incorrect, because they imply that the only good woman is the one that can't talk.

Eaton Hall

The Grosvenors came into possession of land at Eaton, about three miles due south of Chester, in the fifteenth century when they built their first family home there. As their wealth and social rank increased, so the Grosvenors built ever larger houses and these culminated in an enormous mansion designed by Alfred Waterhouse and built between 1870 and 1883. Even the great art historian Nikolaus Pevsner, normally measured in his architectural assessments, described Eaton Hall as a 'Wagnerian palace' and 'the most ambitious instance of Gothic Revival domestic architecture anywhere in the country'. Most of the building was demolished in the 1960s.

The heraldic achievement of the Grosvenors has a red hand on it. The legend tells that there were once two claimants to Eaton Hall and its estates and they decided to have a contest to settle the matter. They are said to have stood on the bank of the Dee and agreed that the one whose hand first touched the land of the Eaton estate which lay on the opposite shore would be the undisputed owner. The first claimant jumped into the river and began to swim as if there was no tomorrow. The other stood coolly on the bank of the river, unsheathed his sword, cut his left hand off and threw it, obviously with his right hand, across the river. The disembodied hand got there before the swimmer and its owner was adjudged the winner – it could be said he won hands down.

Readers may think that this story verges on the apocryphal. The seemingly far-fetched nature of the legend has not prevented occasional reports of the hand – dripping blood, of course – being seen floating about in the air at the spot on the side of the Dee where the contest is said to have taken place. Is it looking to be reunited with the wrist and the rest of its medieval owner?

Ellesmere Port

Ellesmere Port is more or less due north of Chester and perhaps not one of England's most glamorous places. It claims a haunted pub. The behaviour of its ghost is a trifle unusual. To start with, he apparently wears a pin-stripe suit, has hair flopping over his left eye – and on the one occasion he allegedly approached the then landlady with outstretched arms. He disappeared when she screamed, so we are left pondering what its action would have been had she not screamed.

The room in which this strange experience took place was the landlady's bedroom. It turned out that a previous licensee had hanged himself in that room. Did he have a pin-stripe suit and floppy hair?

As if to confirm that there is something uncanny in that bedroom, the dog belonging to a subsequent licensee refused to enter the room but stood at the door looking frightened, growling unhappily with his hackles rising.

Farndon

This attractive village lies on the River Dee almost due south of Chester with a church very badly knocked about in the English Civil War. It has a bridge which joins Cheshire and Wales, built about 1345. On stormy nights, it is said that sounds like those that terror-stricken children would make are heard, apparently emanating from beneath this bridge. They are supposed to the frenzied screams of the two sons of a Welsh prince who were drowned here by English assassins in the fourteenth century. Occasionally small, whitish human figures are seen, thought to be the ghosts of the boys.

Little Sutton

A common theme in stories of the supernatural is that of the phantom hitch-hiker or pillion rider. The basic story with many variations is that a motorist, perhaps dressed in rather out-of-date clothes, picks up a hitch-hiker who talks about himself or herself and then suddenly vanishes, sometimes during the journey or on reaching the destination. The motorist is understandably shaken by this experience and pours it out to his nearest and dearest and, indeed, anyone who will listen. It is then that the motorist learns that the hitch-hiker fits perfectly the description of someone who, some years ago, was killed on the road at exactly the spot where the helpful motorist picked him up.

One variation on the theme is that of a biker who suddenly finds that he is not alone and that he is being accompanied by an uninvited pillion rider who appears from nowhere and disappears equally mysteriously. Sometimes the biker will describe an icy embrace from behind as being the first sign that he is not alone. Just such an experience happened about thirty years ago to a young man from Little Sutton (which is just to the west of Ellesmere Port). He and a mate were both on motorbikes on the A41 going towards Childer Thornton when he realised that he had a female pillion rider. He remembered his first thought being that his unexpected companion seemed to be weightless and made no difference to how the bike handled. When he got home he described her appearance to his mother. In the street lights he had been able to see that she had a blue headscarf, a gap in her front teeth and auburn hair which had streamed out when the bike was in motion.

He seems to have taken this strange episode very stoically. A week later he was visiting an aunt in Liverpool and told her his curious tale. She listened carefully and then took a photograph out of a drawer. It showed the woman he had described and was a distant relation. A year later the gentleman, who still lives at Little Sutton, came off his motorbike – sustaining serious injuries – at exactly the same spot where he first become aware of the girl behind him on the bike.

Neston

Neston in the Wirral is about ten miles north-west of Chester and part of it enjoys extensive views over the estuary of the River Dee and towards the Clwydian Hills.

Perhaps its greatest claim to fame is as the birthplace in 1761 of Emma Hamilton, who went on to immortal fame for the passion she aroused in the breast, and indeed other parts, of Horatio, Lord Nelson, arguably Britain's greatest British naval hero.

The local Catholic church was the scene of a curious incident just before the end of the nineteenth century. A local woman called Teresa Higginson used to take care of the church keys when the priest was away, and she was in the church on one such occasion when she encountered a priest she had never met before. He told her to get things ready because he intended to say Mass. When Mass was over, the priest, who seemed to know his way around, retired to the vestry. The woman cleared up quickly and entered the vestry herself – only to find, to her total astonishment, that everything was in its normal place and that there was no sign of the priest. The vestry only had the one door.

Not frightened but certainly perplexed, Teresa informed the bishop and, from the description she gave, he had no hesitation in saying that the person she had seen was a former incumbent who had died many years earlier and been buried in the churchyard. The explanation given for this strange occurrence was that the priest had perhaps forgotten to say a Mass on someone's behalf and could not rest in peace until he had fulfilled his obligation. The would-be recipient of the Mass had died and the poor priest was therefore doomed to roam forever in his well-meaning but futile attempt to put things right. It could be that Teresa unconsciously had some psychic powers which had been recognised by the priest.

Parkgate

Parkgate in the Wirral is a curious place. It rose and prospered as a port when the silting of the Dee saw the decline of Chester's seagoing trade. Ships left regularly for Ireland and visitors enjoyed the bracing winds to be had on the front. However, just as Canute couldn't command the tides, so no one could prevent the build-up of shifting sands in the Dee estuary. Parkgate found itself marooned, looking over saltings rather than deep water, and now only occasionally is the front lapped by particularly high tides.

A rather benevolent ghost was reported in the 1870s at the Old Quay House in Parkgate, which had once been a pub, later a prison and then a pleasant dwelling house. A middle-aged gentleman moved in with his bed-ridden niece. He was cast in the role of carer but what might otherwise have been a difficult and demanding life was made much easier for him by the ghost of an old woman wearing a red cloak. Her initial arrival was unexpected and uninvited but she was soon welcome because she made many appearances, usefully keeping the niece company and chattering away cheerfully about all manner of topics. For no apparent reason she abruptly stopped her visits, much to the distress of the living occupants of the house.

Sands of the Dee

The River Dee (Afon Dyfrdwy) used to widen out into its estuary further east but for convenience the estuary can now be said to begin at Flint on its south bank. It has become heavily silted, especially on the north, Cheshire or Wirral, shore. The speed of the incoming tides in the estuary has long been notorious and rightly feared and over the years they have taken their toll on the stupid, the foolhardy and the plain unlucky. Many are the stories and legends of those who have been overwhelmed by the tide and swept to their death. The Revd Charles Kingsley (1819-75) chose to commemorate one of these events in the ballad *The Sands of the Dee*. This tells of a young girl called Mary who is instructed to fetch the cattle home on a wild and stormy day but who loses her way and is drowned. Not sparing the melodrama, Kingsley gives us:

…O is it weed, or fish, or floating hair?
A tress of golden hair,
A drowned maiden's hair,
Above the nets at sea;
Was never salmon yet that shone so fair
Among the stakes at Dee.

They rowed her in across the rolling foam,
The cruel crawling foam,
The cruel hungry foam,
To her grave beside the sea!
But still the boatmen hear her call her cattle home
Across the sands of Dee.

It almost goes without saying that in places like Neston, Parkgate and Heswall there were once many (but more recently, far fewer) reports of strange and macabre wailing noises coming from the estuary, especially on storm-ridden nights. Some are even said to resemble the young lady still calling her cows to her.

Saughall

The Greyhound Inn in Saughall, a village in the north-western outer suburbs of Chester, is extensively modernised but dates back in parts to the late fourteenth century. In 2003 and 2004 cleaners working in the pub during the hours it was closed began to complain that they were being attacked by invisible assailants. Then, early in 2004, one of the cleaners saw a ghost. Dressed in clothing of the nineteenth century and sporting a bushy beard, long black coat, and watch-chain, he wasn't short of cheek: when first spotted, he was attempting to pull a pint of beer. The cleaner wasn't short of cheek either – her response was to tell him to 'bugger off'. Perhaps he wasn't used to being talked to like that, because he promptly vanished. Not long after, a stack of stools collapsed in the bar just after staff had tidied up after closing time. They had stacked these stools scores of times before and there seemed to be no rational explanation for why they had suddenly collapsed in the empty bar.

These events attracted the interest of psychic investigators, who brought with them a mass of sophisticated equipment, but it was the age-old tried and tested method of holding a séance which provoked a fine paranormal response. They claim to have established contact with several spirits, including that of a little girl and of three men, one of whom was greatly resented by the others. It was thought to be he who caused a notice firmly attached to the wall to fall off suddenly and with a considerable clatter. The equipment picked up a number of spectral lights and unexplained sounds like voices.

Shocklach

Shocklach is little more than a hamlet in the strangely remote and quiet countryside south of Chester and close to the Welsh border. The parish church of St Edith is a small Norman building. Tradition has it that once a year it presides over a mass ghostly get-together.

Brereton is a well-known family name in Cheshire and once a year all the dead members of the family are said to leave their graves and travel to the church in spectral coaches. So many conveyances gather that the lanes in the vicinity become gridlocked. Curiously, although many people claim to have seen the coaches and carriages making their way towards Shocklach, there have been no reported sightings of them going back after the phantom family confabulation.

Stanney

Near Ellesmere Port this otherwise unexceptional place boasts a ghostly pecking duck. Over the years this spectral bird has proved material enough to make a nuisance of itself by pecking the ankles of passers-by. The pecks are painful.

The duck was enough of a nuisance for an exorcism to be attempted but the creature refused to co-operate and continued assaulting any ankles that ventured too close. Strong suggestions of a wind-up occur when we learn that the village butcher became so fed up with the duck's activities that he grabbed it and cut its head off. This raises the question of how you can decapitate anything as insubstantial as a ghost – even if it is the ghost of a duck. Credulity is stretched even further when we learn that a ghostly headless duck still waddles its way around the district. If it has no head, does it still manage to peck?

Tilstone Fearnall

Tilstone Fearnall is no more than a hamlet on the A51 Chester to Nantwich road. On this road at what is known as 'Haunted Hollow', there have supposedly been some occasional sightings of a fearsome cowled monk described as being about 10ft tall. Not many people would hang around to swap reminiscences with him.

SUGGESTED ITINERARIES

In spite of the fact that central Chester is compact, it is perhaps difficult to do justice to the city and all the supposedly haunted locations by attempting a walking tour of them in one day. Two itineraries are provided here, both of which take in a selection of the haunted sites and while walking these itineraries, many of the city's other interesting 'sights' could be enjoyed with the aid of a good guide book.

Bumbling around a place like Chester stopping suddenly to check the map, or pulling up abruptly on spotting something worth closer scrutiny in crowded streets, invites irritated shoppers and others to hurl abuse. The centre of Chester becomes almost impossibly congested on good weather days between April and the beginning of October. From the explorer's point of view, it is extremely difficult to take in the sights when jostling with other users of the pavement. Little enjoyment is to be had. Frustration follows.

The author's preference when exploring towns is to do so between mid-April and mid-September, when the days are long and early mornings and evenings are light. Fine weather and a fresh morning are an exhilarating combination, and the streets of most cities are relatively uncluttered from, say, 6.30 a.m. until 9.00 a.m.

Between them, these two walks in their different ways provide a very good idea of the diverse character of the centre of Chester.

Walk 1

Starting point: Town Hall

With your back to the Town Hall, turn left and walk along Northgate Street passing the Pied Bull on the left. A few yards further on the same side of Northgate Street is the Blue Bell.

Cross Northgate Street and walk briefly back towards the city centre. Almost immediately turn left through the Little Abbey Gateway following the alleyway through to Abbey Square. Turn left across the Square and at the bottom of Abbey Street, climb the steps to the city walls.

Turn left along the city walls and pass the Phoenix or King Charles's Tower. Continue along the city walls in a westerly direction with the chasm containing the Shropshire Union Canal down below on your right.

At the Northgate, you are close to the site of the Old Gaol. Descend briefly into Upper Northgate Street and you can see the Bridge of Sighs.

Return to the walls and continue along them to Morgan's Mount. Continue along the walls past Bonewaldestnorne's Tower and descend steps to obtain a view looking up at the water tower. Return to Bonewaldestnorne's Tower and proceed along City Walls Road.

Follow City Walls Road noting the Old Chester Royal Infirmary buildings at a slightly higher level on the left. A couple of hundred yards on, also on the left, are the buildings of the Queen's School.

At the Watergate, cross City Walls Road and turn up Watergate Street with No. 102 on your left.

A little distance up Watergate Street, cross the road to the Stanley Palace. Cross Nicholas Street at its junction with Watergate Street and some distance on the right of the street is Watergate's Wine Bar.

Cross Watergate Street at The Cross and turn left up Northgate Street, returning to the Town Hall.

Walk 2

Starting point: Town Hall

With your back to the Town Hall turn right down Watergate Street to The Cross. Go ahead into Bridge Street and almost immediately on the right or west side of the street is the 'Cruise' shop at No. 12 Bridge Street.

A few yards along Bridge Street on the same side is the shop called 'Essentials' (better known to Cestrians as the former 'Barlow's' pub). Continue along the west side of Bridge Street to its junction with Grosvenor Street. Cross Grosvenor Street and the Falcon Inn is facing you.

Go down the west side of Lower Bridge Street and facing you on the other side of the street, almost opposite the Old King's Head is Tudor House.

At the corner of Lower Bridge Street and Castle Street stands the Old King's Head. Turn right into Castle Street and cross at the junction with St Mary's Hill. On the left at the top of the steep part of St Mary's Hill is the Old Rectory.

At the bottom of St Mary's Hill is Shipgate Street. Turn right into Lower Bridge Street and almost immediately on the right hand side is the Bear and Billet. At the Bridgegate, climb the steps to the city walls and proceed eastwards with a grandstand view of the River Dee, the Old Dee Bridge and the Groves.

Continue along the walls until reaching the New Gate. Descend the steps into Pepper Street and on the south side you will see the Pepper Street Chapel. Return to the New Gate.

Continue into St John Street and Little St John Street with the Amphitheatre on the right. Keeping St John's church on your right, go along Vicar's Lane and turn down on the right towards the ruined east end of the church to see the 'coffin in the wall'.

Continue down the path towards the Queen's Park Bridge with the Anchorite Cell on the green to the right. At The Groves, turn right and walk westwards towards the distant Old Dee Bridge. Up on the right the Old Bishop's Palace can be seen.

Turn right up the hill along Souters Lane and at the top, with the Newgate on your left, go on to St John Street. On the right is the Marlbororough Arms.

Turn right into Foregate Street to the junction with Frodsham Street. Cross Foregate Street and at the east corner of the junction is the jewellery shop of W.H. Samuels. Go along Foregate Street towards the Eastgate.

Continue along Eastgate Street and shortly on the north side is Thornton's. On the same side of Eastgate Street, shortly before its junction with Northgate Street, is the Boot Inn.

From the Boot Inn turn right at The Cross into Northgate Street and return to the Town Hall.

BIBLIOGRAPHY

Anonymous, *History of the City of Chester*, 1815

Conway, *Dark Tales of Old Cheshire*, 1994

Coward, T.A., *Picturesque Cheshire*, 1903

Davies, O., *The Haunted: A Social History of Ghosts*, 2007

Emery, G., *Curious Chester*, 1999

Harris, B., *Bartholomew City Guides: Chester*, 1979

Howard, L., *Dark Cheshire*, n.d.

Leigh, E., *Ballads & Legends of Cheshire*, 1861

Marshall, J., *Myths and Legends of Chester*, 1986

Matthews, R., *Haunted Chester*, n.d.

Morriss, R. and Hoverd, K., *The Buildings of Chester*, 1993

Pearson, J., *Haunted Places of Cheshire: On the Trail of the Paranormal*, 2006

Pevsner, N. and Hubbard, E., *The Buildings of England: Cheshire*, 2003

Slemen, T., *Haunted Cheshire*, 1999

Stephens, R., *The Wharncliffe Companion to Chester*. Various editions

Windle, B.C.A., *Chester: A Historical and Topographical Account of the City*, 1903

Woods, F., *Cheshire Ghosts and Legends*, 1990

Woods, F., *Legends and Traditions of Chester*, 1982

Other titles published by The History Press

Haunted Chesterfield

CAROL BRINDLE

From creepy accounts of churches and shops to chilling tales of hospitals, pubs and cinemas, *Haunted Chesterfield* contains a chilling range of ghostly phenomena. Drawing on historical and contemporary sources, you will hear about the ghost child of the Yorkshire Bank, the ghost of George Stephenson at the Pomegranate Theatre, and many more ghostly goings on.

978 07524 4081 1

Haunted Nottingham

ANDREW JAMES WRIGHT

The streets and buildings of Nottingham it seems are alive (if that's the right word to use) with ghosts, ghouls and things that go bump in the night. Haunted Nottingham explores the supernatural side of the city and its surrounding areas and finds many reports of unexplained happenings, weird goings-on and ghostly appearances. The author, Andrew James Wright, has been a ghost investigator for thirty years and has accumulated a vast collection of spooky stories from all over the East Midlands.

978 07524 4194 8

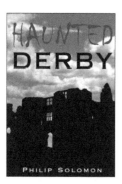

Haunted Derby

PHILIP SOLOMON

Explore the darkest secrets in the history of Derby with this collection of true-life tales from ghost-hunter Philip Solomon. Featuring hooded monks and spectral centurions, the White Lady of Elvaston Castle and a chain-smoking spirit named 'Smokey Joe', his book records all the phantom residents of the ancient city, and provides an intriguing introduction to the hospitals, taverns and streets where 'paranormal becomes normal'.

978 07524 4484 0

Ghost-Hunter's Casebook

BOWEN PEARSE

This is an essential guide to the career of Britain's most eminent ghost hunter, Andrew Green, who investigated hundreds of hauntings during his career. The most important cases from his lifetime of research – each of which has been extensively re-researched and updated by Bowen Pearse, who knew Andrew for many years, and who has complete access to all of his personal papers – are collected together in this volume.

978 07524 4500 7

If you are interested in purchasing other books published by The History Press, or in case you have difficulty finding any History Press books in your local bookshop, you can also place orders directly through our website
www.thehistorypress.co.uk